This is the stuff you've always been embarrassed to ask about the world of modern business.

The *What You Need to Know* books can get you up to speed on a core business subject fast. Whether it's for a new job, a new responsibility, or a meeting with someone you need to impress, these books will give you what you need to get by as someone who knows what they're talking about.

Each book contains:

▶ **What It's all About** – A summary of key points
▶ **Who You Need to Know** – The basics about the key players
▶ **Who Said It** – Quotes from key figures
▶ **What You Need to Read** – Books and online resources for if you want to deepen your knowledge
▶ **If You Only Remember One Thing** – A one-liner of the most important information

You might also want to know:

▶ *What You Need to Know about Economics*
▶ *What You Need to Know about Strategy*
▶ *What You Need to Know about Project Management*
▶ *What You Need to Know about Leadership*
▶ *What You Need to Know about Marketing*

i

WHAT YOU NEED TO KNOW ABOUT BUSINESS

ROGER TRAPP

CAPSTONE

This edition first published 2011
© 2011 Roger Trapp

Registered office
Capstone Publishing Ltd. (A Wiley Company), The Atrium, Southern
Gate, Chichester, West Sussex, PO19 8SQ, United Kingdom

For details of our global editorial offices, for customer services and for
information about how to apply for permission to reuse the copyright
material in this book please see our website at www.wiley.com.

Library of Congress Cataloguing-in-Publication Data applied for.

9780857081155 (paperback), ISBN 9780857081162 (ebook),
ISBN 9780857081179 (epub), ISBN 9780857081186 (emobi)

A catalogue record for this book is available from the British Library.

Set in 10.5 pt New Baskerville by Toppan Best-set Premedia Limited

Printed at TJ International Ltd., Padstow, Great Britain

CONTENTS

INTRODUCTION

Business is big. Well, in fact, it's also small, and medium-sized – and very big. The point is that everybody is talking about it. This is because, increasingly, wherever you work, and whatever you do, you are in all probability in a business. And even if you are not working, you will be affected by business. We are all subject to business, as hospital managers, school teachers and politicians all talk about "performance targets", "metrics" and other bywords of management speak.

Television programmes such as *The Apprentice* and *Dragons' Den* present business as a reality show even though the world they portray is a million miles from most people's average day in the office. On the other hand, the programme actually called *The Office* satirised management mantras and the way business is conducted – in much the same way that the *Dilbert* cartoons make fun of how mundane office life can be.

In truth, business is not generally portrayed in a much better light than it was in the 1970s, when the image of British business in particular was bound up with strikes, poor-quality goods and a general air of hopelessness. Even in America, which has always been more exuberant about business, young people were dismissive of their elders who worked in big companies. And perhaps the most famous television programme about business – *Dallas* – took a particularly cynical view of the machinations of corporate life.

Somehow, though, we see through all that and are inspired by such figures as Virgin Group founder Sir Richard Branson, Microsoft's Bill Gates and Apple chief Steve Jobs. We follow their every move in the hope that some of this stardust will rub off and make us successful in the same way as they have been.

The internet has played an important part in this. At the height of the "dot.com boom" of the late 1990s, everybody was so excited that they felt as if they were missing out if they were not involved in a start-up of some kind and thus eligible for a big pot of stock options. There was an excitement about business that was reminiscent of the exuberance that greeted the development of the railways in the nineteenth century. Established businesses grew so fearful of losing their brightest stars that they smashed hierarchies and threw away dress codes in an attempt to hang on to them. The "technology bubble" burst (and many of those options simply disappeared). But the informality – and hence, for want of a better term, the "funkiness" of business that it unleashed – remains.

Nor has this appeal really been dented by the financial crisis of 2008 and 2009. People may have been outraged by the financial alchemy on New York's Wall Street and in the City of London and by its devastating effects on the wider, "real" economy, but this dissatisfaction has not apparently put people off the idea of business.

Indeed, individuals seem more enthusiastic about non-financial businesses than ever. By the middle of 2010, the passion for the technology gadget company Apple's products had reached such a pitch that queues formed outside its stores whenever a new product became available. Slightly more prosaically, the John Lewis Partnership transformed itself from middle England's dependable department store into a shining example of what a business can be even in difficult times by being truly switched on to the wants of its customers and also apparently by being decent – towards its staff (significantly, partners in the business), its customers and its suppliers. What was once a slightly stuffy purveyor of curtain fabrics and household goods became the subject of a television series and gained many a mention in the newspaper columns of the chattering classes – the sort of publicity that is impossible to buy.

Nor are these the only examples of the passion generated by business today – among customers, employees and senior managers alike. Howard Schultz, head of the global coffee bar chain Starbucks, even called the book he wrote about the company's growth *Pour Your Heart Into It*. Entrepreneur Henry Stewart arguably went further, naming the information technology training company he set up in London a couple of decades ago Happy Computer. The company – despite being in a field that can be less than inspiring – is regularly featured in lists of the best places to work and is even using its experience to help other companies become happier workplaces.

There is clearly an appetite for work to be something more than just a means of earning a living.

This is not necessarily new. For example, Hewlett-Packard, one of the pioneers of the technology industry of which Google is a current star, set out an "HP Way" of doing business and employees would often make decisions based on what they thought "Bill and Dave" (Hewlett and Packard) would do.

Of course, this does not mean that everybody in business is following some cult. But it is definitely true that there is huge enthusiasm for business – among would-be employees as well as among policymakers and the general public. Back in the 1960s, when the London Business School was established, business education was almost unknown in Britain – although it was, of course, available in the United States and elsewhere. Now it is very different. In Britain alone, thousands of people study business and management each year, while a significant proportion of each year's graduates head into some kind of business. And the number of start-ups continues to grow, contributing to there being just under three million businesses in the country in 2008.

In the United States, the Index of Entrepreneurial Activity produced by the Kauffman Foundation, an organisation dedicated to promoting entrepreneurialism, found that 558 000 individuals started new companies in 2009, a 4% rise on the previous year in spite of the recession. In Germany 200 000 small businesses were founded in 2009, according to research by the economic research institute *Institut für Mittelstandsforschung*. Meanwhile, China is showing great enthusiasm for enterprise. The number of Chinese who are either self-employed or working in companies not primarily owned by the state rose from about 8 million in 1992 to nearly 80 million in 2008.

However, attractive and exciting as we now realise it can be, business can also be a confusing place. Not only can its activities often involve complex processes or a mastery of obscure niche markets, the whole language of business can appear arcane and hard to get a grip on. Have you, for example, ever stared at the pages of the "FT" wondering how other people make sense of what looks like Ancient Greek to you? Have you ever nodded in agreement in a meeting even though there are so many acronyms and concepts flying around that you have no idea what is going on? Do you find spreadsheets mesmerising? Is your boss's jargon impenetrable?

If you recognise any of these situations, you are not alone. Few of us have had much introduction to business before we start doing it. Although things are starting to change, there is little about business on the school curriculum. As a result, we tend to muddle along, chiefly through a mixture of bluffing and picking up things as we go along.

This book is here to make life easier. It will take you through the main concepts and terms, ideas and phrases you'll come across in the business world. By the end you will have some understanding of how the stock market works, what all those economists are talking about, why cash is king and why being busy isn't the same as making money.

Balance sheets and profit-and-loss accounts should no longer hold any fear for you. And you should be able to talk strategy just like an MBA. In addition, you will have had an introduction to the "nuts and bolts" of business, the parts (often not too glamorous) that bring alive the vision of the founder or head of the enterprise. No longer should you be caught out by finance experts and their figures.

Nor should you fall foul of the lawyers, for there is also a chapter devoted to the increasingly tough laws that govern the behaviour of those in business, particularly directors of publicly-quoted companies. Some of the mysteries surrounding supply and demand, competition and other theories should be clearer, as should be the pros and cons of globalisation.

You will also have a solid grounding in the skills you need to succeed. You will, for instance, learn about time management, about communication skills and even about how to be a leader.

Quite simply, this book provides an introduction to all that you need to know in order to succeed in business. All you have to do now is get out there and do it. True, there will be plenty of challenges, many of them emanating from beyond the world of business. But it can never have been more true that enterprise is a major part of the solution. As a result, there has surely never been a better – nor a more exciting – time to be in business.

WHAT YOU NEED TO READ

▶ For general information on a whole range of aspects surrounding business, *Business, The Ultimate Resource* (A&C Black) is a very good starting point, as is *The Capstone Encyclopaedia of Business* (Capstone). *Financial Times Handbook of Management* (FT/Prentice Hall) is slightly narrower in scope, but similarly useful.

▶ For advice on starting and/or running a small business, try *Good Small Business Guide* (A&C Black) or Sara Williams' *Financial Times Guide to Business Start Up* (FT/Prentice Hall).

▶ Business, the *Ultimate Resource* also has a website – www.ultimatebusinessresource.com. Among those focused on small businesses are www.Bytestart.co.uk, www.Startups.co.uk and www.yoodoo.biz. In the United States, the magazines *Inc* and *Fast Company* and their websites, www.inc.com, and www.fastcompany.com, are both informative and inspirational.

▶ For information on social enterprises and how to start them – the Social Enterprise Coalition – www.socialenterprise.org.uk.

CHAPTER 1

WHAT IS BUSINESS?

WHAT IT'S ALL ABOUT

- ▶ What business is
- ▶ How business developed
- ▶ What types of business there are
- ▶ How business is changing
- ▶ What the future might look like

WHAT IS BUSINESS?

So, what is this thing called business? Essentially, a business is an enterprise set up to make money through selling goods or services or a mixture of the two. However, this is a bit simplistic. Increasingly, there are governmental bodies and charities that are run increasingly like businesses. At the same time, the picture is becoming blurred by organisations that are set up as businesses but look more like charities, with their aims of being "social enterprises" or "not-for-profits" and righting some social wrong. Business is everywhere.

This is all the more remarkable because until the last decade or so – certainly in Britain, less so in America – "business" was something of a dirty word. "Entrepreneur" was a sort of codeword for "wheeler-dealer".

What has brought about this dramatic change of heart? It is fair to say that a large part of it is the internet, with its promise of limitless possibilities. But there is also a much greater willingness to try things – even when it comes to careers. This is perhaps best illustrated by the numbers of business school graduates rejecting positions with investment banks and large corporations in favour of start-ups. Reinforcing all this is a change in attitude among policy makers. Young people are actively encouraged to start their own businesses for genuine reasons, such as doing good and/or creating wealth.

WHO YOU NEED TO KNOW
Sir Richard Branson

Many of today's business heroes are technology wizards who use a bright idea to launch a successful business. Branson is a more old-fashioned buccaneering type of entrepreneur who has got where he has largely on the strength of his extreme self-confidence and love of challenging the big guy. As such, he has become an inspiration to many would-be business owners and is one of the best-known business people in the world.

His best-known business is Virgin Atlantic Airways, which in the 1980s had the audacity to take on British Airways in the battle for the lucrative trans-Atlantic air travel market. A quarter of a century later, Virgin Atlantic is a major player on the travel scene, with various related holidays operations, but Branson still likes to portray the business as a young upstart battling against the established incumbents.

Branson's Virgin empire started as a mail-order record company (which hit the big time with the unlikely hit "Tubular Bells") and has moved into record shops, cola drinks, publishing, health and beauty, financial services and trains. It has not always been resoundingly successful, but Branson – bearded, long-haired and tie-less even in his 60s – always gives the impression that he is enjoying a great adventure.

A SHORT HISTORY OF BUSINESS

There is nothing new to the realisation that a successful business community is vital to a successful political system. One of the earliest examples of what we now think of as a company was the British East India Company, which was founded by Queen Elizabeth I in 1600 and over the next two-and-a-half centuries became inextricably linked with the growth of the British Empire. Perhaps even more significant were the businesses created at about the same time in the newly colonised North America. Historians cannot quite decide on which came first – Puritanism or Capitalism. But it is clear that the two are closely entwined, particularly in America, where such virtues as subordinating the individual to the group, marshalling resources to achieve a single purpose and a belief in self-help are shared by both creeds.

These early joint stock companies – ventures which raised funds by selling shares to investors who became partners in the enterprise (and thus predecessors to the current quoted companies) – paved the way for the businesses that helped develop the fledgling United States. Among these were railway companies and many types of manufacturing enterprises, which in a short period of time turned a few colonist-farmers into the factory of the world.

Similar developments were taking place in Britain, the birthplace of the Industrial Revolution. By the early twentieth century, the geographical spread of some of the businesses mirrored the reach of the Empire, with names such as Cable & Wireless and the now-defunct Imperial Chemical Industries seen as synonymous with British power and influence.

However, for sheer audacity nothing could beat the American businesses. Beefed up by serving a huge home market, the likes of the consumer goods company Procter & Gamble, the conglomerate ITT and the Ford Motor Company became huge players around the world. They used this strength to build up significant subsidiaries and own more businesses around the world than many people realised, but particularly in Europe, long before the more obvious US invasion that led to McDonald's fast-food restaurants and Starbucks coffee shops appearing in every major city.

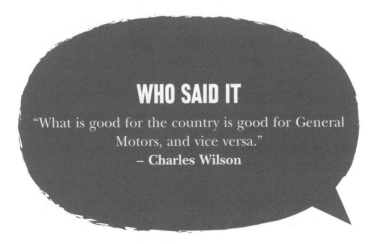

WHO SAID IT

"What is good for the country is good for General Motors, and vice versa."
– **Charles Wilson**

At their peak, these businesses were immense – so big that individuals could, and often did, spend their whole career at a single employer. Thanks to mass production and the application of scientific principles of management established by early business leaders, these businesses were effectively giant machines operating in huge factories employing so many workers that whole towns depended upon and grew up around them. They also developed equally enormous offices to house the people supposedly running them. The rows of machinery minders in the factories were matched by lines of typists and other clerical workers in the offices.

What had started out as exciting enterprises had ballooned into huge bureaucracies where few people really knew what they were doing and why, and where conformity ruled. This is the dull, stultified world of the "Corporate Man", made fun of in films and novels and analysed in the sociological study *The Organisation Man* by William H. Whyte.

This cosy world of golf clubs and long lunch breaks came crashing to an end in the 1970s, when a sudden rise in the oil price by the increasingly assertive oil-producing nations of the Middle East challenged the whole basis on which business in countries such as the United States and Britain was conducted. A serious recession on both sides of the Atlantic paved the way for the arrival of Margaret Thatcher in Britain and Ronald Reagan in America and, with them, a robust "market forces" approach to economics. In the 1980s, a chill wind blew through the boardrooms and across the factory floors of both nations. And, when it was realised that in Germany and Japan, the two nations supposedly defeated in the Second World War, industry was in much better shape, producing better, more reliable products at better prices, a heavy bout of soul-searching set in.

Suddenly, management gurus, notably the charismatic and evangelical Tom Peters, and their theories about "quality", "excellence" and "customer service" were all the rage. In fact, there were so many theories – often contradicting each other – that they were quickly termed fads and ignored by embattled workforces and management teams alike. This was also the period when service industries began to take over in importance from manufacturing. It was the time of deregulation of the financial markets and the arrival of the "Masters of the Universe" on Wall Street and in the City of London. It was also the era of "yuppie" excess. Although nobody at the time realised it was small beer compared with what was to come in the early years of the twenty-first century, it was still seen as unattractive. It was hard to admit to being a merchant banker in polite society.

Despite, or because of, the emphasis on financial engineering at the expense of real engineering, businesses were in no state to cope with the next big recession, which came in the wake of the first Gulf War in the early 1990s. This led to great swathes of job cuts across whole industries that were euphemistically described as "downsizing" or even "rightsizing". It also led to a renewed focus on market forces and the arrival of the term "shareholder value", for a concept designed to improve businesses' focus on their main purpose – making money, or creating value, for shareholders. Conglomerates were "demerged" and "focus" became the watchword.

Business became a lot more efficient. But it also became a lot less enjoyable. The failings exposed by the 1990s recession led to a fresh bout of introspection and the realisation that perhaps business had lost its way.

Some people saw a link between the superiority of Japanese and German goods – particularly in such areas as cars and consumer electronics – and these countries' companies were run differently from the Anglo-Saxon model. In Japan, the concept of a job for life had benefits in loyalty and a readiness to take a long-term view, while Germany had the consensual approach to management common across much of continental Europe, where workers' councils typically had much greater influence than the trade unions in Britain and the United States. However, as time wore on – and Japan and Germany both endured difficult economic periods – the Anglo-Saxon, and, it has to be said, increasingly American, view held sway.

Although some of them drew from other cultures, the gurus and consultants who were growing ever more important in business were largely American. As a result, business premises across the world began to ring with American terms such as "double whammy" and "ball park figure" and managing directors became chief executives or CEOs, a title that Peter Drucker, the guru of gurus, had previously said was peculiar to America.

Some of the analysis of "what went wrong" that followed the early 1990s recession, and the spectacular collapses that accompanied it, took place in Britain. For example,

WHO YOU NEED TO KNOW
Peter Drucker

Peter Drucker was without a doubt the doyen of management gurus. Born in Austria, he moved to the United States in the 1930s and published his first book – an examination of General Motors entitled *Concept of the Corporation* in 1946. Over the next half century he covered a huge variety of management topics, along the way identifying many notions that would become central to business thinking, such as the "knowledge worker" and "managing by objectives".

In the key work *The Practice of Management* (1954) he offered his view of the first principles of management and wrote what has come to be regarded as one of the key statements of management thinking: "There is only one valid definition of business purpose: to create a customer."

Always prolific and provocative, he continued writing and consulting into his 90s and applied the thinking that had originated in the study of large organisations to entrepreneurship and non-profit organisations. But he remained remarkably consistent – the tasks for the manager of the future that he set out towards the end of his life had in fact been identified by him years before.

the Cadbury Committee came up with a code on corporate governance that did much to pave the way for the improvements in that area that have followed, while the Royal Society for the Encouragement of Arts, Manufactures and Commerce (RSA) initiated an inquiry that gave rise to the ongoing experiment with "Tomorrow's Company".

But it was, of course, in America that business was really born again. Particularly in California and in a small area that came to be known as Silicon Valley. The area, close as it is to the prestigious Stanford University and its mighty engineering faculty, had long been a centre for business, giving rise to what would become the computer giant Hewlett-Packard and many others. However, it really came into its own when it became the de facto centre of the world's high-technology businesses. Sure, Microsoft was based in Seattle, a few others came out of the area around Boston and some were even spawned around Cambridge University – Silicon Fen. But the vast majority of the new technology businesses and – more importantly – the new attitudes came out of Silicon Valley.

One aspect of this approach – involving employees or customers in the ownership of the business – had been tried before. Indeed, Britain has at least two long-running success stories in this area – the financial services and retail group the Co-operative Society and the retail company the John Lewis Partnership.

However, it was the first time that a significant group of companies had adopted such an approach. Moreover, it looked so attractive that many other businesses had to start following suit in order to avoid losing their best people.

There has been much comment in recent years about businesses moving away from their original purpose – as expounded by the late Chicago free-market economist Milton Friedman – of being to maximise profits for shareholders. Companies have been encouraged to look

WHO YOU NEED TO KNOW
Charles Handy

Charles Handy is more quietly spoken and more circumspect than many management thinkers. Nevertheless, he has been hugely influential in imagining and describing many aspects of the current workplace.

For example, he developed the "shamrock organisation" as a way of explaining how many businesses would be built around cores of essential executives and workers supported by outside contractors and part-time help. He has also pioneered the concept of the "portfolio career", both in his own way of working and in describing it in a series of accessible and popular books. Reacting against the old split between work and play, Handy sees people dividing their time between work for which they get paid, free work for friends and charities, studying in order to keep up with their professions, working at home and leisure.

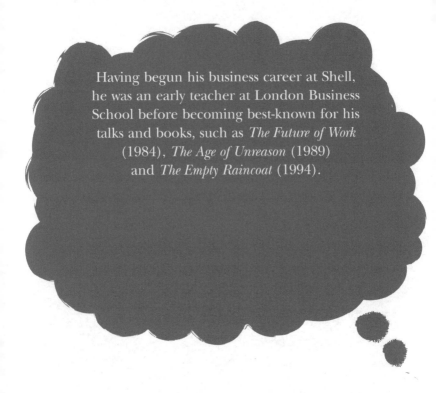

Having begun his business career at Shell, he was an early teacher at London Business School before becoming best-known for his talks and books, such as *The Future of Work* (1984), *The Age of Unreason* (1989) and *The Empty Raincoat* (1994).

at the interests of stakeholders other than shareholders, to engage in corporate social responsibility, even to look for a new form of capitalism.

But what has really made business attractive is that people who previously would not have dreamed of going into commerce suddenly saw it as a way of "making a difference", of getting things done (roles previously answered by public services) and, above all, of having fun.

Having thrown out the notions of loyalty and paternalism in response to market forces, business is now returning to something similar. Companies now queue up to be included in the lists of the best companies to work for, they constantly add to the services they provide for their hard-pressed staff and they encourage them to use mobile technology so that they can work flexibly (critics inevitably say this means working longer). Almost without exception, they are also anxious to stress the good they do in their communities through supporting charities, supplying schools with computers, regenerating rundown areas and the like.

This work hard, play hard approach and almost cult-like devotion to the company that you currently work for harks back to the earliest days of industry, when – just as now – there was a blurring between work and life and a belief that business could change the world. Indeed, Google – towards the end of the first decade of the twenty-first century perhaps the most ubiquitous new company of them all – has been described as "a religion posing as a company".

It is really not going too far to say that business has become a way of life. Which makes this book all the more important.

That said, most people's idea of business – unless they are involved in it – is of the sort of large international affairs that attract coverage in the media through takeovers, strikes or involvement in catastrophe. In truth, though, such businesses are the exception. There are many more businesses that do not attract any attention at all.

Here, we will look at the two main types of business – big business and small and medium-sized business.

BIG BUSINESS

Although they only make up a tiny proportion of the businesses in the world, one could be forgiven for thinking that big companies were the only ones in existence. Most of the coverage in the media is given over to them. And they also attract the greatest criticism from politicians, commentators and the public at large. This is because they are seen as increasingly powerful in a world where ease of communication and other technological developments are enabling more and more companies to act on a global scale.

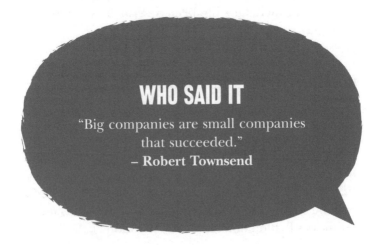

WHO SAID IT

"Big companies are small companies
that succeeded."
– **Robert Townsend**

The most obvious illustration of this is the fact that, thanks to the internet for instance, you no longer have to wait to visit the United States to buy goods from an American retailer. More importantly, large companies are able to make their goods in one part of the world – typically where costs are low – and sell them in another – typically where prices are high. This is globalisation, an increasingly hotly debated issue that will be discussed fully in the next chapter, on the economy.

Some of these large companies are privately-owned. But most of them are publicly-owned. This does not mean that they are controlled by the state – the very opposite, in fact. They are so called because they offer shares that can be bought by the general public through a stock market, such as the London Stock Exchange (LSE), the New York Stock Exchange or the Paris Bourse. In Britain, such companies carry the letters PLC after their name – for public limited company.

The reason why such companies attract so much attention is that – because their shares are publicly traded – the directors are required to make public anything that might influence an investor's decision to buy or sell the shares. Such information includes details of trading, departures or arrivals of key staff and, of course, whether another company has expressed an interest in buying the company (a takeover). Most of the shares in such companies are held by professional investors – "financial institutions", such as insurance companies and pension funds, which have teams of people following the affairs of the companies in which they invest, but individual investors are required to be given the same information. Hence, the pages of news and comment in the serious newspapers.

However, it is not all about simply providing information. As we have seen already, business has become interesting in itself. This is partly because more members of the public are "involved" through owning houses and holding shares (either directly or through their pensions) than used to be the case. But it is also because large companies – and those running them – have become newsworthy like never before. Some chief executives are so familiar that they are almost celebrities. This might to some degree be attributable to the spectacular pay and benefits that some enjoy. But it is also testament to the increasingly important role played by big business in the affairs of everybody. Increasingly, we buy our groceries from multinational supermarket chains, our books, CDs and clothes from international internet companies and our electricity, water and other services from international utilities. Moreover, as the 2008–2009 financial crisis made all too apparent, our banks are not confined to our own high streets. They are becoming more global in reach – and, as such, entwined with each other.

SMALL AND MEDIUM-SIZED BUSINESS

These tend to be private businesses, so-called because they are not owned by outside shareholders who buy and sell an interest in the company through a stock market or stock exchange. Private businesses account for the vast majority of businesses – even if you would not believe it to judge from the amount of media coverage. But avoiding attention is highly attractive to many of the people running these businesses, which range in scale from tiny start-ups to international operations that are the equal in size to many well-known public companies.

Historically, many private businesses, especially in Britain, have "gone public" because such a route offers one of the most effective ways of raising funds for growth. It is also highly attractive because – for the most part – investors leave executives to get on with running the business. However, the increased activity of the venture capital, or private equity, market has enabled many such businesses to obtain the funds they require without having to float the business on the stock exchange. Another route has been for established private businesses to buy all or some of a younger business and so provide the means for expansion. This means that they can continue to enjoy the advantages of being private – particularly the ability to set a strategy that they believe in and do not have to justify to outside shareholders – without worrying about cash. For example, many of the companies that were in the vanguard of using business to further social good were private because their owners were able to take this approach without having to explain it to outsiders. Among these is the California-based outdoor clothing and equipment company Patagonia, whose founder Yvon Chouinard is a committed environmentalist who has for many years pledged that the company give at least 1% of its annual sales to environmental causes.

It is not unheard of for company founders to "float" their businesses on the stock market only to take them private again when they realise that they might have been better off as they were. Sir Richard Branson's Virgin Group is a prime example.

It is fair to say, however, that this problem is not peculiar to public, or quoted, companies. Some companies decide against joining the stock market for fear of losing control only to sell a stake in the business (equity) to a venture capital or private equity business. Since such investors often want to arrange an "exit" within five years or so, this relationship can be just as uncomfortable as the one with the stock market investors.

Private businesses are particularly popular in Germany, where the *Mittelstand*, largely funded by a network of regional banks that often take stakes in the companies, has developed as a powerful alternative to the listed company approach and accounts for much of the country's industrial strength. The United States, too, has a strong tradition of private businesses. Because of the country's vast size, companies can establish highly successful regional businesses with strong links with their local communities away from the attention of the markets. In Asia, there are many business empires, often owned and operated by families, which are highly successful without being publicly listed.

Private businesses take many different forms. A significant proportion of businesses start out literally as one person working from home – and many stay that way. The simplest way for such a business to organise itself is to register as a Sole Trader. The details of what this entails, along with the rules and regulations surrounding other business structures, are more fully discussed in Chapter 3. But in its essence such a form is generally all right for a small business operating from the founder's home, but less appropriate once it grows to include other people and premises.

One of the most common types of private business is the Family Business. Such concerns are the bedrock of enterprise around the world and they range from farms to retail empires. Many of them have grown up to the point where they become large public companies. Many of the world's largest and most successful companies retain a strong family identity. They include Cargill in the United States, Samsung in Korea, LVMH in France, BMW in Germany, Clarks Shoes in the United Kingdom and H&M in Sweden.

The mixing of family and business can be so fraught with issues that it is hardly surprising that so many of the television dramas featuring business centre on family firms. Yet various studies have shown that companies listed on stock markets that have some family ownership outperform those without it.

More than this, however, family businesses are seen to be a good thing in themselves as if they are somehow more worthy than other kinds of business. We talk admiringly of how a favourite shop or supplier is "a nice family business", while even some of the largest businesses continue to stress their family origins and conglomerates often talk of their "families" of businesses.

This slightly unexpected (in a world excited by technology and change) enthusiasm for cosiness and old-fashioned virtues is reflected in the renewed interest in mutuals, co-operatives and community interest companies. Again, the legal aspects of these forms of business will be discussed more fully later. But what is important about them is that they set themselves up as being run for the benefit of their customers rather than outside shareholders.

WHAT YOU NEED TO READ

▶ The fascinating story of how business as we know it has developed over the past few centuries is told in various accounts. Richard Donkin's *The History of Work* (Palgrave) and Anthony Sampson's *Company Man* (Harper

Collins) look at it from the point of view of the people, while *The Company* (Modern Library) by John Micklethwait and Adrian Wooldridge concentrates on the phenomenon of the business entity. Similar territory is covered in the early parts of *The Puritan Gift* (I.B. Tauris) by Kenneth and William Hopper. Niall Ferguson's *The Ascent of Money* (Penguin), from the television series of the same name, is a sweeping account of how finance has oiled the wheels of history.

IF YOU ONLY REMEMBER ONE THING

Business is an essential part of the modern world. Over recent centuries business has evolved to do many things – create wealth, meet human needs and play a part in making the world a better place.

CHAPTER 2
THE ECONOMY

WHAT IT'S ALL ABOUT

- ▶ **What Economics Is and Why It Matters to Business**
- ▶ **Types of Economy**
- ▶ **Markets**
- ▶ **Competition**
- ▶ **The New Economy**
- ▶ **Growth**
- ▶ **Globalisation**

Economists have not enjoyed a good press in recent years. As writer and consultant Diane Coyle explains in *The Soulful Science, What Economists Really Do And Why It Matters*: "The financial crisis has certainly called to account the models conventionally used by banks and hedge funds to assess risk, and the economics profession stands charged as guilty by association."

Yet it is not just the 2008–09 Credit Crunch that has found the economics profession on the defensive. Whenever there is a sudden crisis – or indeed whenever the economy behaves differently than expected – economists come in for criticism for what is perceived to be a limited and overly theoretical view of how the world and, in particular, individuals operate. The success of such books as *Freakonomics* by University of Chicago economist Steven D. Levitt and journalist Stephen J. Dubner and *The Undercover Economist* by Tim Harford may indicate how the so-called dismal science can explain some of the quirks of modern life but they also probably reinforce the view that economists are a pretty strange bunch. After all, analysing complex data to show why people behave in apparently odd ways is not everybody's idea of normal behaviour.

Yet there is no getting away from the fact that a grasp of the basics of economics is essential for success in any type of business. An enterprise that does not appreciate that there is a relationship between supply and demand is doomed to failure. As is the business owner who does not allow a sufficient amount in his or her price for the

WHO YOU NEED TO KNOW
Adam Smith

Adam Smith was a Scottish philosopher who is widely credited with making economics a coherent, standalone discipline. His classic book, *Inquiry into the Nature and Causes of the Wealth of Nations* is a wide-ranging description of the first principles of economics and commerce. Published in 1776, it was immediately successful and is said to have influenced the 1777 and 1778 budgets of British Prime Minister Lord North.

At the centre of Smith's book is the idea of the costs of production. To him, the value of a good was directly related to the cost of producing it. "The real price of everything, what everything really costs to the man who wants to acquire it, is the toil and trouble of acquiring it," he says.

Many regard the book as a sort of right-wing manifesto, citing its description of market forces. However, others stress that it merely sets out some rules governing economic activity. All agree that it has stood the test of time.

cost of producing the good or service. And so is the would-be entrepreneur who prices his or her goods at just above the market rate without offering extra in the way of service.

So, although economics may look dry and theoretical, it is very real in that it effectively sets out the ground rules by which business works. The next few pages will describe the most important of those rules and illustrate how they apply in practice. Once these rules are understood, we can move on to look at growth and the increasingly important issue of globalisation.

WHAT IS AN ECONOMY?

Textbooks describe an economy as a system that attempts to solve the basic economic problem caused by economic resources being scarce while human wants are infinite. Of course, this definition probably raises more questions than it answers. So a few more definitions.

First, Economic Resources. These are resources, or goods, that have a value because they are not freely available. They, of course, include raw materials, fuel and the like. Free goods are those that are available to all, such as – for the moment, at least – air. Water and shelter used to be among them, but the rising world population has made them scarcer. Pollution could do the same for fresh air.

There are a certain number of needs which must be met if people are to survive as human beings. Some of them are material needs, such as food, clothing and shelter. Then there are psychological and emotional needs, such as self-esteem and being loved. They are finite. By contrast, human wants are unlimited. Whether we are farmers in the developing world, factory managers or rich financiers, there are always things that we want more of – food, clothes, bigger houses on the material side and more love, fairness or whatever on the emotional side.

The Basic Economic Problem is caused by the mismatch between resources and want. This forces "economic agents", or those involved in the economy, to make choices. In other words, they have to allocate scarce resources between competing uses. Economics is the study of this allocation of resources. A central part of this is Supply and Demand. Essentially, firms supply goods and services in a range of quantities, depending on the price they can obtain for them. Demand is typically

Demand Curve

influenced by such factors as individuals' incomes, tastes or fashions and changes in prices of other goods.

TYPES OF ECONOMY

So much for the theory. Economies come in various guises. Perhaps the most basic is the one politicians keep referring to when they talk of the nation needing to balance its books – the household economy. Then there are the local economy, the national economy and the international economy. They can be run in different ways, too. So at one extreme is the free market economy, where state intervention is at a minimum, and at the other is the command economy, where the state makes most of the decisions about allocating resources. The United States is the most prominent example of the former, though the extent to which this is true tends to depend upon whether Republicans or Democrats are in the ascendancy. China and Russia have traditionally followed the latter approach, though that is being changed in some respects. The political argument in most democracies, such as Britain and much of Western Europe, centres on how far in which direction to go. But all economic systems face the same economic problem. And this involves deciding what is to be produced, how to go about it and deciding who should benefit from it.

The production process is generally dependent upon the use of three different types of resources. The first of

WHO YOU NEED TO KNOW
JM Keynes

Keynes was a hugely influential economist in his own lifetime, and his importance continues to this day. He made his name in 1919 with the publication of his critique of the terms imposed on Germany after the First World War – *Economic Consequences of the Peace*. His worries turned out to be well-placed. Then in 1936 he published *General Theory of Employment, Interest and Money*, the essential basis for the Keynesian ideas that have proved so powerful for three-quarters of a century.

The book grew out of his concern about the unemployment and poverty resulting from the Great Depression. It was built on his idea that a low level of aggregate demand, or total demand for goods and services in the economy, did not necessarily correct itself and could continue for a long while. This was a challenge to the classical view that wages would fall in a depression to the point where employers would begin to take on labour again and the problem would right itself. He advocated intervention by governments to correct the situation, with expansionary fiscal and monetary policies used to increase demand.

He was also very much involved in the setting up of World Bank and the International Monetary Fund after the Second World War as part of an effort to co-ordinate the international monetary system and improve economic stability.

these Factors of Production is land – not only land itself, but also all the natural resources on it and above and below it, including rainwater, forests and minerals. Second is Labour – or the workforce, while third is Capital. This includes Working Capital – stocks of raw materials as well as goods that are unsold – and Fixed Capital – the stock of factories, plant and machinery, or the things that help turn working capital into finished products. Some economists identify a fourth factor of production – Entrepreneurship. Entrepreneurs are individuals who are different from ordinary workers because of their readiness to take risks – with their own and other people's money – in order to set up new businesses that they hope will make a profit but which could fail, losing them all their money.

Though they are grouped together under resources, not all workers are alike. Each of them has unique characteristics, such as intelligence, skills and attitude. Moreover, education and training can make them more valuable – leading to talk of workers being an organisation's Human Capital, or in the words of many company reports, "our greatest asset".

SPECIALISATION

Another way in which workers can become more valuable is through specialisation. Companies, regions or countries can specialise – so that, for example, some companies only make certain types of cars, while parts of Britain became known for shipbuilding while London is renowned for service industries and some countries have a reputation for particular products, such as the Netherlands and tulips or Japan and miniature electronics gadgets. Globalisation – which is discussed below – is in effect making the specialisation of different countries more intense by making international trade more integrated.

Specialisation by individual workers is known as the division of labour – famously described by Adam Smith in his book *An Enquiry into the Nature and Causes of the Wealth of Nations* by reference to a pin factory. He pointed out that if one worker carried out all the processes – drawing out the wire, straightening it, cutting it, etc – he might be able to make 20 pins a day. But he estimated that 10 workers splitting between them the various tasks could make 48 000 pins. Hence, the chief advantage of specialisation is that it increases output per worker, or Productivity.

This is for a variety of reasons – the specialisation enables workers to become more skilled in a narrow range of tasks than would be the case if they remained jacks-of-all-trades; the division of labour makes it more cost-effective to equip the workers with specialist tools; time is saved by workers not having to move from one task to another; and workers can do jobs to which they are more suited.

However, this division of labour is not without issues. Workers can find their work becoming tedious if they do the same things all day and their quality of work and output may actually decline. Companies, too, can suffer from over-specialising, so that, for example, companies that outsource the production of components can find assembly halted if there are problems in the supply chain, while countries or regions that specialise in certain types of industry can be particularly vulnerable in a downturn.

Just look at subsistence economies around the world to see what life would be like without specialisation.

MARKETS

Specialisation is also one of the building blocks of the modern economic system. Once people stop trying to do everything for themselves they need to set up a system of Exchange. At its most basic, this involves barter – you give me food and I give you shelter, for example. The inconvenience of this led to the development of money – and it was this that helped spur the transformation of economies into the complex organisations that they are today. Money is anything that is widely accepted as payment for goods and/or services or as repayment of debts. It includes coins, notes, cheques and – increasingly – numbers on a computer screen.

The antipathy to bankers and their bonuses that has characterised the years since the 2008 financial crisis is just the latest instance of what the historian Niall Ferguson calls – in his book, *The Ascent of Money, A Financial History of the World* – "a recurrent hostility to finance and financiers, rooted in the idea that those who make their living from lending money are somehow parasitical on the 'real' economic activities of agriculture and manufacturing".

Such hostility has its roots in three notions. First, debtors tend to outnumber creditors, towards whom they tend not to be well-disposed. Second, financial crises and scandals occur often enough to make it appear that finance causes poverty rather than prosperity. Finally, financial services have been "disproportionately provided" by ethnic or religious minorities who have been excluded from owning land or holding public office but have succeeded in finance through their tight-knit networks.

Despite prejudices against it, money has been "the root of most progress", says Ferguson, adding: "Financial innovation has been an indispensable factor in man's advance from wretched subsistence to the giddy heights of material prosperity that so many people know today."

The natural development from money and exchange is a Market. This is simply a place where buyers and sellers meet. Everybody is familiar with the street market, where grocers, butchers and the rest sell their wares to consumers. But there are all kinds of other markets. Anywhere that buyers and sellers come together is a market, whether it is the classified advertisements section of a newspaper, a mail-order catalogue or an internet website. In fact, one of the many ways in which the internet has had a profound effect on the business world is in bringing buyers and sellers together through such businesses such as Amazon, eBay and countless other portals.

One of the most important types of market is, of course, the stock market or stock exchange. It is more like the sort of bazaars where buyers and sellers haggle over prices because – unlike traditional shops and elsewhere – there are no fixed prices. Indeed, it is the movements between the sellers' and buyers' prices that accounts for the indices quoted in the financial news – such as the

WHO SAID IT

"A market consists of all the potential customers sharing a particular need or want who might be willing and able to engage in exchange to satisfy that need or want."

– Philip Kotler

FTSE 100 in Britain and the Dow Jones in the United States – moving up or down. Such movements are down to fluctuations in another staple of economic theory – Supply and Demand. Ask a stock market analyst why the market has gone up on a given day and he will glibly tell you: "More buyers than sellers". When the market goes down it is obviously the other way around. In other words, when demand exceeds supply, prices go up, while when supply exceeds demand they go down. Of course, the questioner really wants to know what is driving these changes in demand. But that is the subject of another discussion (see Chapter 4).

For now, a market where prices for goods (shares) change frequently – not just daily but several times within the day – can be seen as a prime example of the perfect market beloved of economists. It is because of the importance of protecting the integrity of the market that regulators around the world are so keen to stamp out a practice – now illegal – called "insider dealing". This results from some people in the market using confidential information that others do not have to trade shares and so gain an advantage over others in the market through having "imperfect knowledge".

Economists identify various different kinds of market, depending on how buyers and sellers interact together. For example, supermarkets might be deemed to compete with each other mostly in the area of household grocery shopping. But in some respects they will also compete with convenience stores and specialist food stores. Increasingly, they can also be seen to be important players in such areas as selling newspapers and magazines, flowers and petrol and even clothes and household furnishings. As such, they can be seen to be in several different markets at once.

There are further complications. In this age of globalisation (see below), a market might not be governed by national boundaries. For example, English rugby clubs have claimed that they are at a disadvantage in European competition because they are bound by a cap on salaries that prevents them attracting the best players when some of their rivals are not. Alternatively, an international company may have research and development based in one country, part manufacture in another and assembly in still another. In such a case it may not be obvious where its market is and who are its rivals.

WHO YOU NEED TO KNOW
Milton Friedman

Milton Friedman was an American economist based at the University of Chicago who essentially took the opposite view to Keynes. A devotee of the free market, he took the view that governments should not intervene in the economy and involve themselves in business decisions.

He won the Nobel Prize for Economics in 1976, for work concerning the relationship between the growth of the money stock and inflation. He also came up with an explanation for the tendency of countries in the 1970s to experience growing unemployment at the same time as inflation (stagflation) that was based on the concept of the non-accelerating inflation rate of unemployment and long-run relationship between inflation and unemployment (the long-run Phillips curve).

His view of monetary policy as the means of controlling inflation was adopted by the Conservative government of Margaret Thatcher and also followed by President Ronald Reagan. Those who followed his monetary policy became known as monetarists and took up a stance on the role of governments in dealing with unemployment in opposition to the Keynesians.

In addition, as we have seen, the internet is having a profound effect on how business is conducted, and so how markets work. It not only facilitates the splitting up of functions between different parts of the world through enabling swift communication between them, it is actually disrupting markets through what is known as Disintermediation. This is the process whereby steps in the supply chain are removed. This "cutting out the middleman" began in banking in the 1960s when, as a result of changes to government regulations, consumers began investing directly in securities (stocks and bonds) rather than leaving their money in savings accounts, which were then used as the basis of banks' investments in the securities markets. This has accelerated lately with many individuals using the internet to carry out all their banking online without visiting their branches at all.

Disintermediation was largely confined to the banking sector until the 1990s and the arrival of the internet made it easier for consumers to deal directly with suppliers. Among the markets most affected have been the travel industry, where holidaymakers can now deal direct with airlines, car hire companies and hotels and so organise their own trips without having to use the services of a travel agent; and the computer industry itself, where companies such as Dell supply hardware direct to consumers.

Effective markets are vital for there to be the competition on which advances in business, and so improvements in the lot of consumers, depend. There is an old adage that all business people seek a monopoly (on the basis that that would mean that they had seen off their competition and could therefore charge what they liked). But that presupposes a world without regulators dedicated to ensuring there is sufficient competition.

COMPETITION

Economists regard a competitive market as having several different characteristics. The first is that there must be a number of firms in the industry. "Perfect competition" is deemed to exist where there are many firms with none of them large enough to exert economic power over the industry. For example, in the UK farming industry even the biggest "agribusinesses" only account for a small fraction of total output and therefore cannot affect prices. In other industries, there is "Imperfect competition". This tends to be because the market is dominated by a small number of players and can take several forms, including monopoly, oligopoly and others that are detailed later in this chapter. In practice, this applies to many markets, particularly those – such as telecommunications providers and industrial manufacturing – where the heavy initial capital investment makes it impractical for there to be many competitors.

The second centres on "barriers to entry". Generally, high barriers to entry – such as the high cost of production or legal or regulatory hurdles to overcome – reduce competition. One reason for the large number of different retail outlets – independents as well as chains – in the UK is that the barriers to entry are low. Just about anybody with an idea and the money to rent premises and to buy a little stock can open a shop. By contrast, opening a pharmacy, say, requires a licence, while starting a car factory entails extensive investment in plant.

A third requirement for a competitive market is that customers enjoy a "wide choice" of suppliers selling broadly similar products. Commodities, such as steel, oil and basic chemicals, are classic examples of these homogenous goods. Where suppliers claim their products are different from those of their competitors – as in household cleaners and other areas of the "fast-moving consumer goods" market – they use branding to differentiate them. And this helps to create an imperfectly competitive market.

Fourth is "knowledge". In a perfectly competitive industry, there is perfect knowledge – meaning that everybody has access to the same information. There are no trade secrets. Of course, businesses of all kinds are constantly striving to ensure that they have an advantage over their rivals – some special production technique, route to market, etc – on the grounds that this is the way to avoid being in a commoditised market. Indeed, investors are often wooed on the basis of such claims. Perhaps the most notable instance of imperfect knowledge is the secret formula used to make the original Coca-Cola. Known only to a few at the company, it is at least in part responsible for the company being one of the most valuable brands in business history.

All this is important because market structure is deemed to affect the way firms behave. Where there is perfect competition in that there is free entry and goods are identical it is assumed that all firms will charge the same prices. Because the goods are identical any attempt by one supplier to increase prices would lead to an increase in demand at other firms. Conversely, a drop in price by one firm would take demand away from the others, with the result that they would have to cut prices or risk going out of business.

WHO SAID IT

"Competition generates energy, rewards winners and punishes losers. It is therefore the fuel for the economy."
– **Charles Handy**

Of course, prices would not reach zero because firms will only supply goods if they can make a profit. The minimum profit that a firm must make to prevent it shifting its economic resources into making something else is known as "normal profit".

If firms in an industry where there is perfect competition are able to make greater than normal profits – or "abnormal profits" – other firms will be attracted to join the industry. The problem with this is that they will increase the supply and drive prices down. Accordingly, the long-run equilibrium price will be just high enough for a firm to make normal profits, so that no firms are being forced out of the industry and no firms are being attracted into it.

Another effect of perfect competition is that firms will produce at the lowest average cost. This is because if one firm had a higher cost base than its competitors it would still have to charge the same as the others or risk going out of business. Because it would therefore be making less than the normal profit, that is, the minimum profit required for the owners to keep their resources in this sector, it would leave the industry.

If one firm went the other way – making an abnormal profit because it could produce at lower cost, the others would be able to use the perfect knowledge in the industry in order to catch up and match whatever the abnormally profitable firm was doing in the way of using new production techniques, say. In the long run, the costs would be the same across the industry.

By contrast, in imperfectly competitive industries the market structure is seen as limiting competition. Because each firm is producing slightly different branded products it has greater freedom to decide the price. Even if other firms charge lower prices it is not forced to follow suit because it may feel that enough customers will stay loyal to its brand. The higher the barriers to entry, the fewer competitors there are likely to be and therefore the higher prices are likely to be – and the greater the abnormal profits.

This is not to say that imperfect competition is always bad for consumers. Perfect competition may make firms more efficient by making them produce at lowest average cost. But this pressure may not encourage them to be innovative and so better at producing what customers want.

This is particularly true of a market such as that for consumer electronics. A small number of players – mostly well-known brands – compete for early adoption by technologically-savvy buyers through incorporating new features derived from their special knowledge and inventions. In a perfectly competitive market where each player had equal access to the same knowledge there would be little incentive to make the big investments in time and resources required. Consumers might benefit from small decreases in prices brought about by refined production techniques and the like. But they would not see the big gains that a company such as Sony or Apple is able to offer through extensive investment in research and development protected by patents and copyrights. They are prepared to pay a premium price – or contribute to abnormal profits – to gain early access to a desirable product.

MONOPOLIES, OLIGOPOLIES AND THE REST

A monopoly is a market structure that is the opposite of perfect competition. This is because there is only one producer or seller for a product, so that in effect the business amounts to the whole industry.

The situation results from there being barriers to entry, such as high costs associated with setting up in the industry. Sometimes, though, the barriers to entry can be imposed by government when it wants to control an industry, as is the case with Saudi Arabia and its oil industry. Or it may be that the industry is just too important or too complex to be broken up. Even after the trend to privatise state assets that started in Britain in the 1980s and spread around many parts of the world, it was realised that it was impractical to have competition in certain areas. For example, in the electricity industry competition was introduced in the generation and supply areas, but the means by which the electricity was moved around was kept as a monopoly. Similarly, in the rail industry there is some competition between the companies that transport the passengers, but the network is controlled by one entity.

An effective monopoly can also result where one company has exclusive access to a market. This can happen in the pharmaceuticals market when an individual company comes up with a "blockbuster" drug that uniquely tackles a particular condition and is able to protect its position through a copyright or patent – as was the case with the US drugs company Pfizer and the Viagra impotence treatment.

An oligopoly is where there are a few companies competing with each other. Most markets are effectively oligopolistic in that most industries in Western Europe and the United States at least are dominated by a few suppliers. If anything, the tendency has been enhanced in recent years as companies have retreated from markets in which they were not major players. For example, the US industrial giant General Electric under the leadership of Jack Welch made it a policy to retain only those businesses that were number one or two in their markets.

Because it is so commonplace, oligopoly is perhaps the most important theory of the firm. However, economists cannot agree on which model best explains how it works. For now, all we need to know is that for a market to be an oligopoly, supply must be concentrated in the hands of relatively few companies. In addition, those companies must be interdependent so that if, for instance, one company decides to increase sales by dropping prices those increased sales will be at the expense of at least one other company. Finally, there need to be barriers to entry. Without them, other companies would enter the market to gain from the abnormal profits available and would take market share off those already there.

In some markets, the tables are turned so that there might be many sellers of goods or services but only one buyer (a monopsony) or many sellers and only a handful of buyers (an oligopsony). An example of a monopsony might be a universal healthcare system where the government is the only buyer of healthcare services. Alternatively, in agriculture there might be only one food-processor buying from many farmers. An example of an oligopsony would be the media industry (at least until the advent of file-sharing and other aspects of the internet revolution), where a handful of major multi-media conglomerates buy the output of many musicians, writers and other artists. Another example would be the fast-food industry, where a small number of companies, arguably effectively control the market for beef and so can dictate the price that farmers receive.

Obviously, business is far too complex and liable to change to conform exactly to economists' theories. So hybrid definitions have emerged to describe situations observed by academics. This is particularly true of Imperfect Competition, which – as its name suggests – is a hybrid structure where there are at least two providers of goods or services (and hence competition) and competition is imperfect because the products sold by one firm are not identical to those of another.

What are called the neo-classical theories of perfect competition and monopoly were developed in the late nineteenth century, when most industries were characterised by a large number of small firms making identical or broadly similar products. These days, though, fewer and fewer industries are perfectly competitive. Consequently, a number of theories have emerged to explain what happens in more and more markets. One of the most important is Monopolistic Competition, developed in the 1930s in the United States and Britain.

The theory is similar to that of perfect competition – there are many buyers and sellers, each relatively small and acting independently, and there are no barriers to entry. The difference, though, is that the companies produce differentiated goods. Examples of such markets are restaurants, clothing retail and the like. The companies are offering broadly similar products – food, clothes or whatever – but consumers perceive that they have differences that are not just about price.

Though some understanding of the thinking behind theories of competition is helpful, it is not necessary for the business person to become too preoccupied with it. What is important from a business point of view is what happens when it is decided – usually by government-appointed regulators – that there is a competition "problem".

Obviously, monopolies and oligopolies and their various variants are tolerated in certain circumstances, as we have seen with utilities and similar industries. But that tolerance is subject to conditions. For example, water companies in Britain (which enjoy local monopolies) are only allowed to raise prices by reference to a formula linked to inflation. Similarly, the European Commission has acted to ensure that mobile telecommunications companies do not charge their customers too much for being able to use their phones in more than one country (roaming charges).

The key issue is that the company that enjoys a monopoly or dominant position does not abuse it, for example by forcing customers to pay unreasonable prices. Just what amounts to abuse of a dominant position is set out in legislation enacted in many countries around the world, including the United States and Britain, and is covered in the next chapter, on the rules affecting business.

Unsurprisingly, this area has produced some hard-fought and long-running disputes as competition authorities have sought to curb the power of big companies and they in turn have battled to protect interests they believe are the result of their business acumen or investment in research and development or a combination of the two.

For example, Microsoft has been subject to lengthy investigations by competition authorities on both sides of the Atlantic as a result of its perceived dominance of the market for the software on which personal computers run. A particular concern of the European Commission was the Seattle-based company's tying of its Internet Explorer web browser to its Windows operating system. As a result, from March 2010 Microsoft has been required to offer customers in Europe the opportunity to make a free choice of web browser by means of a browser choice screen that pops up when the user goes onto the internet. The Commission believes that the arrangement, running for five years, will encourage innovation in the market and lead to developments in related areas.

Innovation – or worries that it would be less attractive – was also behind the Commission's decision in 2009 to fine the microchip maker Intel more than Euro 1bn. The

Commission found that the company – that is renowned for having the slogan "Intel Inside" stuck on millions of personal computers around the world – had indulged in anticompetitive behaviour through making hidden payments to computer makers on condition that they bought nearly all their microprocessors from Intel and through paying computer makers to stop or delay products containing competitors' chips.

At the same time, however, governments and other officials are mindful of the need to encourage companies to invest in developing new products and realise that they will be less inclined to do this if they do not at least enjoy some period of grace before the competition or another new entrant catches up or passes them.

THE NEW ECONOMY

It is interesting that some computer companies have been tangled up in legislation that has its origins in the attempts to control traditional big business, such as the oil companies, steel makers and railroads that culminated in the antitrust laws introduced in the early years of the twentieth century. For it was the information technology industry – and particularly the part associated with the internet – that at about the turn of the Millennium threatened traditional ways of looking at economics. According to the new thinking, the internet had pushed out old theories of how firms worked and replaced the focus on making money with chasing "clicks", or visitors to their websites. There were some spectacularly successful market flotations as entrepreneurs won over investors excited by the novelty of the concept, but by the time the bubble burst in 2001 many companies had "burned" through their venture capital finance before turning a profit and so crashed.

The good news is that the old rules appear to hold true again. Especially in the years since the credit crisis ended a long period of easy cheap finance. The bad news – in some ways – is that the internet is still there – and still disrupting the way that business is done. As well as being a boon to consumers, who are seeing prices driven down through greater transparency, it provides many opportunities for business. But there is no mistaking that it also brings many challenges.

Perhaps the chief issue is finding a way to charge realistic sums for things that people value. As technology has become ever more powerful and cheaper, people have come to expect more for less. Mobile phone companies effectively give customers the latest smart phones if they sign up for contracts and – if they agree to certain terms – a cheap computer is thrown in as well. Newspapers, which have seen their classified advertising revenues migrate to the web, are being given away for free while their executives seek to find ways of charging for online content that they originally gave away in the grip of the internet fever that struck the business world.

Various commentators – notably Chris Anderson of *Wired* magazine and author of the book *Free: The Future of a Radical Price* – suggest that the old economy could yet be killed off.

GROWTH

It might appear that we have dealt with some big issues so far in this chapter. But in economic terms they have been relatively limited. This is because individual markets come under the title of Microeconomics. The major issues – inflation, unemployment and other matters that keep finance ministers awake at night – are described as Macroeconomics. When politicians or commentators talk about "the economy" they are essentially referring to macroeconomics.

At the centre of these issues is growth, which is something like apple pie to economists; everybody wants it. Economic growth, or the rate of change of output, is calculated by reference to an internationally-agreed measure of output called Gross Domestic Product, or GDP. This enables the performance of national economies to be compared with each other and with the past.

The most basic reason why a rise in GDP, or economic growth, is seen to be a good thing is that the economists' assumption that wants are infinite leads individuals to feel better if they consume more this year than they did

Gross Domestic Product of Selection of Leading
Economies (in $bn at current prices and purchasing
power parities)

	2005	2006	2007	2008	2009
France	1869.4	1953.4	2072.5	2120.0	2080.3
Germany	2586.5	2710.2	2853.2	2909.7	2818.3
Italy	1649.4	1739.8	1841.6	1866.5	1789.7
Spain	1188.1	1306.1	1412.1	1434.2	1398.5
UK	1971.3	2065.1	2131.5	2186.5	2110.4
US	12579.7	13336.2	14010.8	14369.4	14185.2
Japan	3872.8	4080.4	4297.5	4358.3	4144.5

(Source: OECD Annual National Accounts database)

WHO SAID IT

"Start with the idea that you can't repeal the laws
of economics. Even if they are inconvenient."
– Larry Summers

last year. As politicians the world over realise, people want to be better off this year than they were last year.

Economic growth is also good for nations because they are interdependent with others around the world. Much like a household, a national economy must sell to other countries about as much as it buys from them. This is known as the Balance of Trade and it is generally better for it to be in surplus rather than deficit.

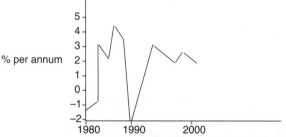

Economic growth rates fluctuate over the course of the economic cycle.
(Source: OECD Economic Outlook)

When the economy is growing at a reasonable rate, the people running it are generally happy because a number of good things follow. More people are employed – which is good for the individuals concerned and good for economists because it means that scarce resources are not being wasted, tax receipts rise because more people are working, while social security and related costs fall and businesses thrive because individuals have greater spending power. This in turn leads to further tax receipts because businesses are taxed on their profits. Assuming there is no underlying debt to pay off, the government of the day's finances are in good order and it can invest in the sorts of things that make the country a better place in which to live – roads, public services and the rest.

Matters only begin to turn sour if growth is too rapid, fuelling Inflation. This is calculated in a few slightly different ways but is essentially the rate of change of average prices in an economy over a given period. Inflation is generally a worry because rising prices erode the value of savings, so that consumers, for instance, need more money to buy the same things. Rising prices also cause confusion and uncertainty in markets. Inflation is generally reckoned to be under control if it is at or under about 5% a year. It was a major problem in many countries, including Britain and the United States, in the 1970s and 1980s. In 1975, UK inflation topped 24%. But this is nothing like the levels seen in Argentina and Brazil in the 1980s or in Zimbabwe more recently, when prices were rising by hundreds of per cent a year.

Conversely, a lack of economic growth – as in a Recession or Depression – is bad. Lack of demand for goods and services means that people lose their jobs (if there is also a recession in places where the country trades there can also be a rising trade deficit because of the failure to sell goods abroad). Rising unemployment is clearly miserable for the individuals involved, but it is also bad for the economy because it is a waste of resources and can create structural problems that can take years to put right. In addition, in the sort of modern economy that has a welfare system that supports people who are out of work such a turnaround can quickly have a detrimental effect on the national finances because tax receipts will fall off before those running the economy have a chance to adjust public spending.

Just as countries want to grow so do the individual companies operating within them. There are several reasons for this. Those listed on stock markets are expected to grow because investors want to see their returns improve from year to year. The companies want to grow because those running them are typically ambitious and – like sports people – want to see how good they can be. In addition, they are conscious that they are generally operating in highly competitive markets. As a result, standing still or "bumbling along" is rarely an option. It is usually a choice between press on or be overtaken and possibly taken over or taken out.

Companies grow in two main ways. They can grow through internal growth or organically (by increasing output through extra investment or a larger workforce) and they can achieve external growth through acquisition, that is, a merger or a takeover.

In a merger the boards of directors of the two companies agree – with the support of the shareholders – to join their companies together. In a takeover, it is clear from the outset that one company is the senior partner. (Many mergers are presented as a coming together of equals but soon become more like takeovers.) Takeovers can be amicable in that the board of the target company agrees the price with the acquiring company and then recommends that shareholders accept the terms. But some are contested. This means that a battle for control of the company can follow, sometimes with another bidder involved. In such a case, certain rules come into play regarding the timetable of the bid and the acquirer needs to win just over 50% of the shares in order to gain control.

There have been numerous studies showing that many mergers and acquisitions fail to meet the objectives set for them. And yet executives continue to seek deals. Why? The key arguments are that a larger company may be better able to exploit economies of scale; that a larger company may be better able to control its markets; and that a larger company may be able to reduce its risk. This last point helps to explain conglomerates. These collections of diverse companies go in and out of fashion a little but their raison d'etre is that a company that has a portfolio of interests spread among different sectors is better able than more focused companies to withstand the ups and down of the economic cycle. For example, a building products business might do very well in a boom but be among the first to suffer in a downturn, so its parent company might try to diversify into an industry that is more resistant to harsher economic conditions, such as a retail chain offering cheaper goods. Interestingly, tobacco companies in the 1970s and 1980s diversified into insurance and other industries because they were concerned about the effect the increasing antipathy to smoking might have on their industry, only to find that in recent years their core business has been something of a cash cow.

Regardless of the effect on the fortunes of the companies involved, there are wider concerns. Because mergers tend to reduce competition they can give rise to investigations by the competition regulators keen to avoid the creation of the conditions that can lead to monopolies, oligopolies or cartels. (The ramifications of such investigations are discussed in the chapter on the Rules of Business.)

But there is a complicating factor – government involvement. In some countries, notably France, there has been a policy of creating "national champions" by encouraging firms to merge on the grounds that this serves the national interest. Some countries also have restrictions on who can own utilities and other businesses seen to be of national strategic importance.

It is a controversial area. Not least because of the supposed move towards free trade around the world discussed in the next section on globalisation. Suffice to say that it is likely to remain murky for some time to come.

GLOBALISATION

It is hard to believe now, but just a generation ago, you actually had to visit another country in order to experience its culture, eat its food or buy its products. Sure, the influence of the United States loomed large over most of the world – largely through its central position in the worlds of film and popular music but the lifestyle depicted was hard to share in since only a handful of iconic items, such as Coca-Cola and Levi's jeans, made it across the Atlantic or the Pacific to overseas consumer markets. Even within Europe, products stayed within their national boundaries. For instance, Germans drove Opels, Volkswagens and Mercedes, French drivers had Citroens, Peugeots and Renaults, while the British made do with Austins, Morrises and Rovers. Cars from other countries were seen as very exotic indeed. Now they are commonplace.

What has happened in the intervening years is a rapid escalation in a process known as "globalisation". Thanks to the internet and other technological developments, the rise of international travel and the trend for media to be truly international rather than local, we are all a lot more cosmopolitan and sophisticated than our immediate forebears. The world has become a lot smaller – and a lot less diverse. Visit just about any city in the world and not only can you watch CNN or BBC News in your hotel room but you can also go down in the street and go shopping in Zara, Benetton or The Gap. When you get tired, you can stop for a McDonald's or a Starbucks.

However, attractive as all this may be it is not the whole story. The world is also a lot more integrated than it used to be. The financial crisis that began in 2008 was so serious partly because in the world – and particularly its financial institutions – there is so much interconnection. Round-the-clock reporting of business ensures that what happens in a stock market on one side of the world automatically feeds into one on the other. There is little chance for those involved to pause and take stock.

However, while this is seen as a bad thing in times of crisis, it is generally highly attractive for consumers and provides opportunities for business that simply did not exist a while ago. Globalisation enables a whole range of businesses, from clothing retailers, through electronics companies to financial services firms, to become more competitive by having some parts of their operations – garment making, circuit board assembly, call centres, for example – carried out in developing countries.

Of course, this phenomenon – to the extent that it involves sourcing raw materials or goods overseas – has been around for centuries. In the Roman, Greek and other empires, trade was a highly important element, while further east the development of the Silk Road and the Spice trade can be seen as early versions of the trade routes that today bring fresh vegetables to our supermarkets around the year. Later on, the British

Empire and then the Commonwealth supplied a range of raw materials and also created a ready market for British goods and services.

However, in its current form it really began in the early 1980s, after Theodore Levitt, a professor of marketing, wrote an article in the *Harvard Business Review* under the title "The Globalisation of Markets". He predicted "the emergence of global markets for standardised products on a previously unimagined scale of magnitude".

This spurred multinational companies to reverse an earlier trend for giving their overseas offshoots the freedom to develop regional businesses in favour of creating massive global brands. As a result, each business sector is dominated by just a handful of universally-recognised names. Companies such as Nike, Coca-Cola, Nestle, Mercedes and Apple are familiar throughout the world.

The idea has become more sophisticated lately, with some acknowledgement of a need for local differences within the global brands. For example, the Japanese car makers Toyota and Nissan tailor different models to different parts of the world by making them in local plants.

Equally, there has been a realisation that globalisation is not just about the development of mega-brands. In his best-selling book, *The World Is Flat*, Thomas L. Friedman argues that the latest phase of globalisation began at about the start of the current millennium and is driven by the ability of individuals to collaborate and compete globally. The enabler of this is what he calls the "flat-world platform" created by "the convergence of the personal computer (which allowed every individual suddenly to become the author of his or her own content in digital form) with fibre-optic cable (which suddenly allowed all those individuals to access more and more digital content around the world for next to nothing) with the rise of work flow software (which enabled individuals all over the world to collaborate on that same digital content from anywhere, regardless of the distances between them)."

Globalisation has not been without its critics. Protests at the 1999 World Trade Organisation talks in Seattle and subsequent events aimed to highlight how workers in the developing world were not benefiting as much from free trade as the big corporations they served. The theme was taken up in such books as *No Logo* by journalist Naomi Klein and *Globalization and its Discontents* by Joseph Stiglitz, the Nobel Prize-winning former chief economist at the World Bank. Stiglitz says he wrote his book because while at the bank he saw "firsthand the devastating effect that globalisation can have on developing countries, and especially the poor within those countries".

However, he goes on to point out that he believes globalisation "can be a force for good and that it has the *potential* to enrich everyone in the world, particularly the poor". For this to happen, there will have to be changes to the way the process has been managed, including to the trade agreements and policies that control it, he writes.

Since Stiglitz's book was written, there have already been changes. Most important, globalisation is no longer the preserve of large western companies. Aided in part by the upheaval caused by the Financial Crisis, businesses in China and India and other "emerging markets" are starting to assert themselves on the world stage. To take just a couple of examples, China's Geely car maker has bought the Swedish company Volvo, while India's Tata Motors has acquired Britain's Jaguar and Land Rover. These developments are likely to be followed by many more, both involving these two rising economic powers and other countries, such as Brazil and other Latin American nations.

At the same time, some of the western companies that were in the vanguard of the globalisation movement are starting to realise that the "one size fits all" approach is unlikely to work in the long term. Some of the changes are largely about retailers, say, introducing a variety of formats on the basis that there is a thin line between familiarity and ubiquity. Others are about shifts in management structures, so that international businesses are less likely to be centrally governed. After all, the internet and other technological advances mean that new types of organisation are emerging all the time.

Whatever shape it takes in the future, globalisation is unlikely to run out of steam. Indeed, the development of new-look global businesses is likely to be closely tied with the reconsideration of the role of the State in the Economy that in many parts of the world will characterise the coming years.

The fall of Communism in 1989 was widely seen as proof that the controlled economy could not compete with free markets, while the Financial Crisis of 20 years later led many to question whether the answer was really unfettered markets. Combine this with the huge public deficits run up by many western economies and growing concerns about the ability to finance pensions and other social benefits and it is clear that new thinking is required. Traditionally, the drive to find solutions of this type has come from business. As can be seen by the many innova-tions that have appeared in the field of "Cleantech" – broadly, businesses dealing with such environmental challenges as finding renewable energy sources and dealing with waste – there is no reason to believe this will not continue to be the case. As a result, the opportunities for business are perhaps greater than ever.

WHAT YOU NEED TO READ

▶ There are countless textbooks and guides to the foundations of economics, some of them simpler than others. *Economics* by Alain Anderton (Causeway Press) and *A-Z Handbook Economics* by Nancy Wall (Philip Allan Updates) – are useful introductions.

▶ There are also increasing numbers of *Freakonomics*-type books. Of these, Tim Harford's *The Undercover Economist* and *The Logic of Life* (both Abacus paperbacks) are entertaining and accessible. John Kay is also highly informative, in books such as *The Truth About Markets* (Penguin) and *Everlasting Lightbulbs, How economics illuminates the world* (Erasmus Press).

▶ In the wake of the financial crisis, the workings of the world's financial markets have been much discussed. John Kay's *The Long and The Short of It, finance and investment for normally intelligent people who are not in the industry* (Erasmus Press) does what its title suggests, while Nassim Nicholas Taleb's *The Black Swan* (Penguin) and *Fooled By Randomness* offer original views on how markets work, while JK

Galbraith's *The Great Crash 1929* and Nobel Prize winner Paul Krugman's *The Return of Depression Economics* (both Penguin) offer some historical perspective.

▶ Globalisation has been much debated in recent years and there are plenty of books setting out the various views. Among the most prominent are Thomas L Friedman's *The World Is Flat* (Penguin), Joseph Stiglitz's *Globalization and Its Discontents* (Penguin) and Naomi Klein's *No Logo* (Flamingo). Energy expert Jeff Rubin's *Why Your World Is About To Get A Whole Lot Smaller* (Virgin) is also worth consulting, while Diane Coyle's *The Weightless World* (Capstone) was one of the first attempts to explain how technology was changing everything.

IF YOU ONLY REMEMBER ONE THING

Market forces like supply and demand, competition and the need for growth affect everything that happens in businesses of every shape and size.

CHAPTER 3
THE LAWS

WHAT'S IT ALL ABOUT ➡

▶ **Different Types of Business and The Rules Affecting Them**

▶ **Insolvency and Bankruptcy**

▶ **Employment Law**

▶ **Directors' Responsibilities**

Generally speaking, the laws governing business become more complex as the organisation grows. Accordingly, there are few laws – other than those affecting private citizens – concerning the most basic form of business, the sole trader, rather more for incorporated businesses and a lot more for companies that are listed on a stock market. International businesses of all sizes, of course, have to understand the laws of the countries in which they are trading. These can be markedly different in fact and in interpretation from those in a business's home-land and so those running such businesses need to be wary. For example, executives of companies engaging in internet gambling found themselves arrested in the United States after the US government suddenly cracked down the activity in 2006.

WHO SAID IT

"It is the rule of rules, and the general law of all laws, that every person should observe those of the place where he is."
– Montaigne

The laws for different types of business set out below apply in Britain. While those in other countries will be roughly equivalent, anybody seeking to work in business overseas or to expand a British business overseas needs to carry out proper research.

SOLE TRADER

To set up as a sole trader, all that is required is for the business owner to inform the tax authorities that he or she is self-employed and they can then start trading right away (provided they have obtained any licences or other authorisation that their area of business might require). An additional advantage is that there is no need to register with Companies House or to file accounts there. However, the sole trader is totally liable if anything goes wrong.

LIMITED COMPANY

Many businesses either start off as or quickly incorporate to become Limited Companies. Not to be confused with PLCs, limited companies enable business owners to separate their business and personal finances and so limit their liability if the company fails. Private limited companies cannot offer their shares for sale on the stock market, but they can have shareholders as well as directors. Such shareholders would share responsibility with the directors should anything go wrong, although, again, their personal assets would not be at risk. Limited companies are subject to corporation tax on their profits, while sole traders pay income tax under the self-assessment scheme.

PARTNERSHIP

Partnerships are similar to sole traders in that the partners are personally liable for any debts, meaning that any personal assets as well as what is invested in the partnership are at risk if the business runs into trouble. The idea is that the partners share the risks and liabilities, the management and any profits from the business. As such, this can be a better approach than being a sole trader because the responsibility and work is shared, but it can also be worse in that one partner's livelihood and indeed lifestyle can be put at risk by the actions of another partner. Accordingly, legal advisers urge people to only form partnerships with those whom they trust and can work with and who also bring something to the business venture. Those seeking a partner purely as a means of gaining extra finance might be better advised to go to their bank.

LIMITED LIABILITY PARTNERSHIP

Like sole traders, private partnerships have not been subject to the sort of rules on financial disclosure that govern limited companies. However, the increasingly litigious nature of modern business – particularly against accounting firms that have been felt to have been less thorough than expected in their auditing of companies that have subsequently got into trouble – has led to the development of a new business structure, the Limited Liability Partnership. The LLP retains the flexibility of a partnership rather than the more structured organisation of a company, but shares with companies the limited liability of individuals (its chief attraction) and similar filing and disclosure requirements (its chief disadvantage in the eyes of many professionals).

PUBLIC LIMITED COMPANY

A public limited company is a company that can sell shares to the public, usually through a recognised stock market (see Chapter 2). British public companies are designated by having the letters PLC after their names. In the United States, the equivalent is Corporation, while in France and Spain it is SA, and in Germany it is AG.

In Britain, a company wishing to be listed on the stock market has to have an issued share capital of at least £ 50 000 (or the equivalent in euros), with at least a quarter of that paid up. As in other countries, companies that become public are subject to more stringent controls than their private counterparts. This is to protect investors and to ensure that trading in the shares is fair.

The most obvious difference is that public companies have to submit much more detailed accounts than private businesses. Connected with this is the requirement for them to publicise any events that could affect the value of the company, such as the departure of key staff, important contracts and litigation.

There are also clear rules on how public companies should conduct acquisitions of other companies. In Britain, there is a takeover code administered by the Takeover Panel, which is drawn from heavyweights working in the City of London. Among other things, the rules require all shareholders to be offered the same deal, rather than those with major blocks of shares being offered preferential treatment. They also set out the timetables for bids and the conditions under which they are either abandoned or have to be accepted.

Public companies are also subject to stricter rules on such matters as making loans to directors and the sale and purchase of their shares. They are even required by law to have a company secretary and to hold an annual general meeting. Private companies need have neither.

LISTED COMPANY

Listed companies are public companies that have their shares listed or quoted or traded on public stock markets, such as the London Stock Exchange, the Paris Bourse or the New York Stock Exchange. There are also other public markets, such as the Alternative Investment Market in London (for companies that do not meet the criteria for a full listing) and Nasdaq, a US market specialising in high-technology stocks.

HOLDING COMPANY

Sometimes companies form part of a group. Depending on the structure the executives decide to adopt, the component companies can act individually (often trading under separate names so that only the initiated or the readers of fine print realise they are part of the same group) or they can operate effectively as arms of a single company. If the former approach is taken, it is common for there to be a holding company that does not really participate in the activities but instead operates as a sort of central command, supplying expertise in such areas as human resources and finance to the operating companies.

There are rules on what constitutes a subsidiary and on the relationship between a subsidiary and a holding company is set out in legislation such as the British Companies Act. Much of the application of these rules has to do with tax, since – although the trading structure adopted should be "tax neutral" – there can be advantages to keeping activities separate or lumping them together depending on the circumstances.

COMPANY LIMITED BY GUARANTEE

Companies limited by guarantee are generally found in the not-for-profit sector, although there is no restriction of what type of business can be structured in this way and sometimes conventional companies will adopt such an entity for a club or sports association that is not part of its normal business.

The key legal distinction of such a company is that it has guarantors rather than shareholders. The guarantors are members who agree to make a limited contribution towards paying off the company's debts if it is wound up. However, the amount is usually fixed at a nominal £ 1 and is only payable if there are insufficient assets.

CO-OPERATIVE

A co-operative is a business owned and controlled by the people working in it. In Britain, the best-known example is the Co-operative Society, which has grown from roots in the industrial towns of northern England to become a familiar face in retail and financial services around the country. But co-operatives are also common among the agricultural communities of such countries as France and Italy and in business sectors around the world. The cocoa growers of Ghana who supply the Fairtrade chocolate company Divine are co-operative members.

For a while co-operatives went out of fashion – there was even an attempt in the 1990s to take over the Co-operative Society – but they have been making a comeback.

Similar to the co-operative is the Mutual, which is owned by its members and, as its name suggests, exists for the benefit of a wider community rather than shareholders. Mutuals were at the heart of the building society movement, which was set up to give people of limited income the opportunity to save for their own homes. Like co-operatives, mutuals went into decline, and many were taken over by quoted companies or "demutualised" and turned into banks. In the wake of the financial crisis, however, they have become more popular again.

So much for the structure. The differences between the various types of business might look complex and hard to distinguish. But, frankly, deciding on the form the business should take is the easy part. There is now so much legislation governing just about all activities of business that all those involved – but particularly directors of public companies – must be extremely wary.

The following pages will offer some guidance for dealing with this burden. Rather than providing a detailed breakdown of the law in all the areas that concern people in business, the rest of this chapter will point to areas of potential trouble where all business people, from new recruits to experienced directors, need to be careful. The key is if in doubt seek legal advice, or at least consult a reference book like those quoted here.

INSOLVENCY AND BANKRUPTCY

Probably the biggest fear facing a business owner or director is what happens if it all goes wrong. As is clear from the discussion of the contrasting liabilities associated with different business structures, the effect on the individual depends upon the type of business with which he or she is involved.

It is important at the outset to appreciate the difference between insolvency and bankruptcy. They are not interchangeable terms. Insolvency is usually applied to businesses rather than individuals and takes two forms. The first is cash-flow insolvency and means the inability to pay debts as they fall due. The second is balance-sheet insolvency, which is where liabilities are greater than assets. A business may be cash-flow insolvent but balance-sheet solvent if it holds illiquid assets that it cannot easily turn into cash and so pay off debts. Equally, it could be balance-sheet insolvent but still be cash-flow solvent because, although its assets are outweighed by liabilities, it has enough revenue to meet its debts. This can be the case if it has long-term debt, and many businesses are in this situation for much of the time.

Bankruptcy, on the other hand, is a status determined by a court of law as a result of insolvency. It generally leads to legal orders intended to deal with the problem.

Directors of a company that runs into financial difficulty generally find themselves in something of a dilemma.

WHO YOU NEED TO KNOW
Enron

Enron was the obscure energy trader that over 15 years grew into America's seventh largest company, employing more than 21 000 people in more than 40 countries before collapsing in late 2001. Its collapse after huge deceptions involving fictitious profits and concealment of debts was a prime factor in the passing in 2002 of the Sarbanes-Oxley Act in an attempt to plug accounting loopholes. The demise of the company led to the conviction of former senior executives on securities fraud and related charges and also brought about the collapse of the accounting firm Arthur Andersen.

A false picture of profitability and growth was also behind the collapse of the telecommunications company WorldCom, which in July 2002 became the largest filing for bankruptcy protection in US history. It was eventually found to have had debts of $ 11bn. Company founder Bernard Ebbers was sentenced to 25 years for the fraud.

Essentially, they must steer a path between the natural optimism that comes with being in business and despairing that there is nothing to be done when often there are options available.

It is particularly important to realise that, while directors generally have to act in the interests of shareholders overall, if the company becomes insolvent or even looks as if it may do so their first responsibility is to the creditors. In addition, directors may be personally liable for wrongful trading if it can be shown that they knew or ought to have realised that there was no realistic chance of the business continuing but carried on as normal.

This is the sort of thing that keeps people awake at night. The good news is that, while businesses do fail, the consequences are not always dire. Indeed, it is often possible for restructuring or turnaround specialists to find a way out of the problem. After all, much as mortgage lenders do not readily call in loans on families that cannot make their payments, so banks do not lightly write off their loans to businesses. Hence all the reports in the business pages of the newspapers of company boards in talks with their bankers over rescheduling debt, refinancing or the like.

EMPLOYMENT LAW

Other than having to do their book-keeping and work out their taxes, the first contact most businesses have with the law is when they take on their first employee. Hiring an extra person opens up a host of legal issues right from the start. Indeed, even the recruitment process can be fraught since in many countries, including Britain and the United States, there are rules about how advertisements may be worded and interviews can be conducted in order to avoid discrimination. Then, once the successful candidate has been hired, they must receive a contract of employment setting out the details of the job as well as information about pay and benefits. Employers also need to compute and collect the tax payable by their employees and to keep records of their employees' absences, sickness, disputes and disciplinary issues. This is particularly important if they end up dismissing any of them since there are strict rules relating to dismissal. Thousands of cases claiming unfair dismissal go to employment tribunals every year in Britain alone.

Finally, employers have a "duty of care" towards anyone working for them and so must ensure that they are working in a safe environment and are not exposed to possible health and safety hazards. In order not to fall foul of increasingly wide-ranging health and safety legislation, directors and managers need to be aware of the need to assess risk in the workplace regularly.

CORPORATE MANSLAUGHTER

Sometimes, a health and safety issue can be so serious that it results in loss of life. And it is becoming increasingly likely that senior managers will be held accountable by the courts. For example, Britain now has a Corporate Manslaughter and Corporate Homicide Act, which came into force in 2008. It provides that broad failure of management rather than individual failings can be prosecuted.

This is a major break from the past, when bringing corporate manslaughter or corporate homicide cases against companies proved difficult largely because of the tests the prosecution had to pass – proving that a single individual was guilty of gross negligence and that this individual was the "controlling mind" of the company. Small companies, which tended to be controlled by one person, were more easily caught than larger organisations, where responsibility was more likely to be split between various people. A convicted organisation can be subject to an unlimited fine, plus either or both of an order requiring it to take steps within a certain time to remedy the situation and anything resulting from it that was a cause of death and possible change procedures or systems; and an order requiring the organisation to publicise the fact that it has been convicted as well as the particulars of the offence and the fine and remedial order if made.

COMPETITION AND CARTELS

There has been a tightening up of the laws on competition and cartels, too, with regulators around the world increasingly tough on companies thought to be behaving in anti-competitive ways through taking part in cartels, abusing dominant market positions and other practices. The cases brought against Microsoft and Intel discussed in the previous chapter are indicative of how seriously this issue is being treated.

BRIBERY AND CORRUPTION

Bribery and corruption, long a grey area for businesses involved in certain industries and operating in certain parts of the world, has also been subject to a crackdown. In 2010, Britain passed a Bribery Act in accordance with its support for an Organisation for Economic Co-operation and Development convention against corruption. Countries across the world have backed the convention in "combating bribery of foreign public officials in international business transactions" and so are required to pass legislation making their support into an effective bar on the practice.

THE ROLE OF THE BOARD

However, none of these developments has attracted the kind of attention given to the increasing amounts of regulation and guidance surrounding Corporate Governance. Whenever there is a high-profile corporate collapse, a spectacular fraud or a banking crisis, there are calls for a tightening of rules, stricter codes of practice and changes to the regulatory regime. Recent years have seen such a reaction to the recession of the early 1990s, the collapses of Enron and WorldCom in the early 2000s and, most recently, the financial crisis.

At the time of writing, the full extent of the new-style regime in the banking sector is not known. But directors across the United States and indeed in any company dealing with the United States are fully aware of the reach of the Sarbanes-Oxley Act. Popularly named for the two US legislators who sponsored it, the Public Company Accounting Reforms and Investor Protection Act of 2002 was passed to close the loopholes that more creative accountants had exploited so effectively in order to over-state profits and understate liabilities and so prevent investors seeing the true state of the businesses concerned.

The Act has caused great concern because of its wide scope. It applies to all companies, whether incorporated in the United States or not, that issue public securities in the United States and file reports with the US Securities and Exchange Commission. That obviously includes the growing number of companies that are listed in New York as well as on their home stock exchanges. It can also cover subsidiaries.

Among the chief provisions are that the chief executive and chief financial officer must certify the annual and quarterly reports. Those who knowingly sign false

WHO YOU NEED TO KNOW
Paul Sarbanes
Michael Oxley

Paul Sarbanes and Michael Oxley are the US legislators who sponsored the legislation that became the Sarbanes-Oxley Act, which was signed into law by President George W. Bush in July 2002. Sarbanes, a Democrat Senator from Maryland, and Oxley, a Republican Congressman from Ohio, each introduced legislation in their own houses that became the Public Company Accounting Reforms and Investor Protection Act of 2002, better known as Sarbanes-Oxley or Sox. Sarbanes was the longest-serving Senator in Maryland history, representing the state from 1976 to 2006. He had previously been a member of the House of Representatives and in 1974 was involved in the first steps to impeach President Richard Nixon. Oxley had worked for the FBI before entering politics in 1972 as a member of the Ohio House of Representatives. He was elected a US Representative for Ohio in 1981 and, like Sarbanes, served until 2006.

statements are liable to fines and severe criminal penalties. They could also forfeit bonuses and awards of shares. In addition, management must report on their internal controls and procedures for financial reporting in the annual reports filed with the SEC.

It is because directors and managers in subsidiaries in Britain and elsewhere may also have to produce similar reports in this and other areas that there has been such widespread concern about the legislation. Essentially, all businesses potentially covered by the Act are well advised to take a safety-first approach. In particular, internal controls and procedures in overseas subsidiaries should mirror those in the US parent company.

In Britain what is expected of directors is set out clearly in the Companies Act 2006, and this is augmented by the Financial Reporting Council's UK Corporate Governance Code, the most recent version of which came into force in mid-2010.

The latest legislation marks a departure because for the first time the duties of directors in all companies are spelt out. Before, the law was unclear. There were anachronisms, contradictions and plenty of uncertainty.

However, as *The Director's Handbook* stresses, the new Act is "more than a consolidation or simplification of what had gone before. There were some subtle changes to the rules, and Parliament introduced a new concept: 'enlightened shareholder value'."

This amounts to an instruction to directors to look beyond the interests of the company and its shareholders and take account of other factors that might affect a company's success.

The Act sets out seven duties. Three are concerned with conflicts of interest. The other four are:

Duty to act within your powers – This is designed to prevent directors furthering their own narrow interests rather than those of the company. For example, directors can use their power to issue new shares to raise capital for the company rather than to keep control in friendly hands by distributing shares to friends and cronies.

Duty to promote the success of the company – This is a change from the old law requiring directors to act in good faith in the best interests of the company as a whole. Now, they must act in a way they consider, in good faith, would be most likely to promote the success of the company for the benefit of its members as a whole.

To fulfil this duty, directors must have regard to six factors that demonstrate "responsible business behaviour". There is no requirement to value one factor over another. The directors might even discount all six. The board just needs to be able to demonstrate that it has given reasonable consideration to them. The six factors are the likely long-term consequences of any decision, the interests of employees, the need to foster business relationships with suppliers, customers and others, the impact of the company's operations on the community and the environment, the desirability of maintaining a reputation for high standards of business conduct and the need to act fairly between all members.

Duty to exercise independent judgment – Irrespective of the circumstances in which a director is appointed, he or she is required to act in the best interests of the company as a whole rather than represent one shareholder or a group of investors.

Duty to exercise reasonable care, skill and diligence – This is designed to get away from the idea that a directorship is some kind of honorary position. Even unpaid part-time non-executive directors are required to treat being a director as a proper job.

WHO SAID IT

"A verbal contract isn't worth the paper it's printed on."
– **Samuel Goldwyn**

This ties in with the defined roles for chairmen and those on audit and remuneration committees. It is acknowledged that non-executive directors may not have access to the same information as full-time executives, but they are expected to use their wide experience to ask the right questions and to challenge executives. In doing this, they will be expected to use their professional skills and knowledge.

Directors of UK-listed companies are also required to comply with the UK Corporate Governance Code. Although the code is not legally binding, its provisions are seen as best practice and there is a certain pressure to comply. Companies that do not comply are required to explain why not. Ignoring the code is not an option.

With regulators mindful of instances where powerful chief executives have apparently been able to pursue strategies almost unchecked, the code puts greater emphasis on the role of the chairman. In particular, it states that the chairman and chief executive should not be the same person. Although it is accepted that there might be certain exceptions, it is not recommended that the retiring chief executive should become chairman.

There is also a requirement that companies carry out annual reviews of the effectiveness of their internal controls and risk management systems, while – in keeping with the Financial Services Authority's Remuneration Code – there are also statements of best practice regarding bonuses, shares and other aspects of remuneration.

With so many codes and laws, it is easy to be confused. Moreover, there are serious penalties should directors get it wrong. They range from fines and dismissal to being disqualified from being a director. They can even be imprisoned for agreeing to take part in cartels.

However, lawyers insist that provided directors understand their responsibilities and take reasonable steps to protect themselves they should not be unduly worried.

WHAT YOU NEED TO READ

▶ Practical information on dealing with the rules and regulations of business is provided in David Impey and Nicholas Montague, *Running a Limited Company* (Jordans), while *The Director's Handbook* (Institute of Directors/ Kogan Page) is an indispensable guide for executives of all sorts of business. Colin Barrow's *The 30 Day MBA* (Kogan Page) is also helpful in putting it in context.

▶ There are also detailed guides to the workings of the City of London, such as Philip Coggan's *The Money Machine: How the City Works* (Penguin) and Alexander Davidson's *How The City Really Works* (Kogan Page), similar books about Wall Street and plenty of guides to corporate governance. Christine Mallin's *Corporate Governance* (OUP) is notable for its inclusion of governance issues in such rising economies as Brazil, China and India.

IF YOU ONLY REMEMBER ONE THING

The long arm of the law reaches into many areas of business. It determines everything from the structure of the company to how companies compete, and the rights of employees.

CHAPTER 4

THE NUMBERS

WHAT IT'S ALL ABOUT

- ▶ **What Accounts Are**
- ▶ **The Difference between Cash and Profit**
- ▶ **What The Balance Sheet Tells You**
- ▶ **Types of Finance**
- ▶ **Taxes**
- ▶ **Different Measures**

Successful businesses are about a lot of things. Vision, commitment, desire, passion, fun – and a lot else besides. But ultimately if the numbers do not work then neither does the business itself. It follows from this that for an individual to enjoy success in business he or she must have at least some basic understanding of the numbers – and how they relate to the success or otherwise of the business.

Many people – even those who have been in business for some time – claim not to really understand the financial side of the business. They say that they are in sales or production or whatever and that they leave the financial side of things to the accountants or the finance department.

This is dangerous for a number of reasons. First, the more people who understand the basics of the business, the better. By understanding the effect of actions within the business on the numbers – be they cash flow, profits or even share price – they can see the warning signs of trouble and act accordingly. Second, not understanding the numbers gives too much power to those who do (or think they do). Having a strong grip on the financial side enables managers to challenge others' plans or ideas and improves their chances of succeeding with their own. In the well-run organisation every business decision will take at least some account of the financial aspects. Third, and this follows from the second point, an individual with an understanding of the numbers will inevitably do well in the business – particularly if that is combined with flair in another area, such as marketing or sales.

Think of understanding finance as a basic building block for a career in business – whatever size or type of organisation you work in. Just as the basic economics covered in an earlier chapter should help you understand the context in which businesses operate, so the coming pages should assist you in making sense of the numbers that come up all the time in any business. By the end you will be able to tell cash flow from profits, distinguish the bottom line from the top line and understand the different forms of profits. You should even be able to understand your tax bill.

ACCOUNTING

For as long as there have been businesses of any kind, the people running them have attempted to keep some kind of record of how they are faring. Indeed, double-entry book-keeping – the concept of each transaction being recorded as a credit and a debit in order to ensure accuracy that is the basis of accounting – has been traced back to an Italian monk, Luca Pacioli. Record keeping of this kind involves recording whatever is put into the business and everything that is taken out, hopefully showing that the output exceeds the inputs.

Since Pacioli's day, accounting has become somewhat more complex, with increasing numbers of regulations (not all of which are agreed upon by every major economy) but the essence remains the same. The

WHO YOU NEED TO KNOW
Luca Pacioli

Luca Pacioli is regarded as one of the greatest if least known figures of the Renaissance. Born to a poor family in Tuscany, Pacioli joined a Franciscan monastery and became apprenticed to a local businessman. However, his love of mathematics led him to abandon that for a life of scholarship. In 1494, he published his *Collected Knowledge of Arithmetic, Geometry, Proportion and Proportionality*, which set out to address what he saw as the poor mathematics teaching of the time. However, the work became famous for the section that was a treatise on accounting. In it, Pacioli described double-entry book-keeping, also known as the Venetian method and the technique that is the basis of modern accounting. In so doing, he assured a place for himself in history as the "father of accounting".

He was also ahead of his time. For, not only did the ledgers he described closely resemble the layout of accounts today, but his book was written as a sort of "how to" guide for business people.

purpose is to establish what the business owns in terms of assets, to establish what a business owes in terms of liabilities, and to establish what the profitability was at certain times and how it was obtained.

There are certain widely-agreed rules that govern how companies set out their accounts and record their assets and liabilities. However, different countries have historically developed their own rules, known as financial reporting or accounting standards, so that, for example, there are the Statements of Standard Accounting Practice (SSAPs) in Britain and Generally Accepted Accounting Principles (GAAP) in the US. This was confusing enough when business was more bounded by national boundaries, but in the era of globalisation it makes little sense. So an International Accounting Standards Board has been set up with the aim of producing rules that will apply across the world. Its greatest challenge has been agreeing its approach with the existing national standards setters, but progress has been made and those involved are hopeful that there should be "convergence" between the international standards and the national standards of leading industrial countries in the coming years.

Although it deals with numbers and requires a certain precision from its practitioners, accounting is not an exact science. The room there was for interpretation was laid bare in the 1990s by *Accounting For Growth*, a book in which then City analyst Terry Smith suggested that the impressive growth in profits seen by many British companies in the late 1980s and early 1990s could be put down to manipulation of the figures or "creative accounting". Such practices were not illegal, but they could be sufficiently misleading so that great steps were taken in the following years to tighten the terms of accounting standards. As a result, bald abuses are really no longer possible. But there is still room for interpretation – within the rules laid down by the standard setters.

So it is important to realise what accounts do tell you and what they do not. For a start, they do not reflect everything that could affect a business. Only matters that can be assigned a monetary value appear in the accounts. Accordingly, things like the arrival of a rival business, while important, will not appear on the balance sheet.

Second, they are not there to benefit anybody other than the business. The accounts are not meant to tell the shareholders or the bankers who have provided funds how the business is doing. Rather they are just a record – for those running the business (who may or may not be the owners) – of assets and liabilities.

Assets are usually entered into the accounts at the cost at the date they were purchased. This is in keeping with the convention of the conservative approach to accounting. However, assets that are recognised as changing in value from time to time, such as freehold land and buildings, will be revalued at intervals and the cost, or market value (whichever is lower) will be entered in line with the conservatism principle.

WHO YOU NEED TO KNOW
Arthur Andersen

Arthur Andersen was an accounting firm that began life in 1913 in the US city of Chicago as Andersen, DeLany & Co, after its founders Arthur Andersen and Clarence DeLany. It became Arthur Andersen in 1918 and already had a close relationship with the beer company Joseph Schlitz Brewing Company. From the start, the firm was dedicated to training and education as ways of competing with its rivals. It became famous for its training centre outside Chicago and for the rigour with which recruits were developed.

The firm grew quickly, but – unlike its rivals, which developed ever more complex names as they merged with and took over rivals – it was always simply known as Arthur Andersen. Highly successful and highly profitable, it was looked upon with a certain envy by others in the field. But it was also regarded by many as being more aggressive and single-minded in its pursuit of clients.

Although it was later cleared of wrong doing, the firm was never able to regain the reputation lost through its association with the creative accounting techniques and other financial deceptions carried out by the energy company Enron.

Depreciation is a term that frequently comes up in a discussion of accounts and assets. It is simply how accountants show an asset being used or consumed over its working life, to reflect that something with a finite life, such as a piece of equipment or a vehicle, will not be as valuable after a few years as it was when new.

Going concern is another term that is used frequently. It refers to the convention that accounting reports assume that a business will continue trading indefinitely. The assets are seen as a means of generating profits rather than as for sale.

Although accounts are not drawn up for the use of anybody but those running the business, it is clear that others are interested in them. This is particularly so if the company is listed on a stock exchange or has outside shareholders. It is for this reason that all but the smallest private companies are required by law to have their accounts audited each year. The biggest public companies must submit their accounts to a rigorous process conducted by auditors from one of the large international accounting firms.

This process is constantly being reviewed and – following the high-profile collapses of the energy trader Enron and the telecommunications company WorldCom after complex frauds came to light – particularly tough rules were introduced in the United States and in Britain. In the United States, the legislation is the Public Company Accounting Reforms and Investor Protection Act of 2002 – better known as the Sarbanes-Oxley Act, after the two US legislators who sponsored it. The British version is the Companies Act 2006.

CASH FLOW

There is a saying in business that profit is vanity and cash flow is sanity. This reflects the reality that any business – no matter how good it looks on paper – relies on a flow of cash to keep going. Cash is precisely that – cash or certain securities that are regarded as being as good as cash. Profit, on the other hand, is simply a measurement meaning that sales revenue is bigger than expenses and costs.

This looks straightforward enough until you realise that most businesses have to pay for their raw materials, labour and the rest long before they are paid for the finished goods or services. Hence the emphasis on cash. Without it a business will find it hard to buy the raw materials and pay for the labour to generate future revenues.

This lag can be handled with the help of a bank overdraft or other finance. But in the early days, businesses often underestimate the costs they are going to incur before receiving any revenue and, as a result, they can often face closure before they have really got going. Such failure is often the result of Overtrading, a term that is much used by bankers and private equity investors when assessing businesses and essentially means that a firm is trading beyond its financial resources. If they become involved early enough business turnaround experts can save such businesses by focusing on cash flows and reducing unnec-essary expenditure (indeed, often cutting all but essen-tial spending until the business is on a secure footing).

The confusion between profit and cash is clear when people talk about businesses being essentially sound, but just having a cash-flow problem. This is something like the young professional with good prospects not quite managing to make his or her pay cheque last until the end of the month. In both situations, the only answer is a severe cutback in spending and/or a cash injection. In the case of the young professional the cash usually comes from a parent or similarly benevolent individual. With the business it can be bank finance of some kind – an overdraft or a loan, cash provided by an outside investor or money arising from a takeover. Whichever solution is opted for, the decision usually has to be taken quickly since cash-flow problems can escalate swiftly. In fact, the better a business appears to be doing in terms of sales the worse its cash-flow deficit can become. This was one of the problems with the dot.com boom of the late 1990s and early 2000s. Even some of the less esoteric internet-based businesses spent piles of cash before they received the revenues necessary to replenish it and so found themselves in trouble.

Part of the problem is that businesses – especially new businesses, but also established ones – often confine their future planning to preparing a business plan, or budget. This is usually essential for obtaining backing from a bank or other investors and can give the managers something concrete against which to measure their progress. But it is often insufficiently detailed, especially when it comes to cash generation. A budget or business plan is with its attempt to predict future sales, costs and profits in effect often little more than a wish list.

Businesses looking for better control over their cash opt for another planning process known as cash-flow forecasting. Since the typical business plan will not include the purchase of new assets or the payment of outstanding loans, a cash-flow forecast should start with an opening cash balance. To this would be added cash due from customers, while payments to suppliers, the cost of new equipment and other costs, such as promotional expenses, would be subtracted. Then other receipts, such as payments for deliveries, and costs, such as interest payments and tax bills, would be indicated when they were expected to occur. This would then enable the managers to arrive at a projected closing cash balance.

Far from being a theoretical exercise, this could make the difference between success and failure because it would enable managers to see problems arising before they ran out of cash. Anticipating problems enables the business to either alter course or seek assistance in the form of additional funds.

THE BALANCE SHEET AND OTHER CHARTS

It is because success or failure can turn on such apparently small things as having money in the bank at the right time – especially when economic conditions become uncertain – that business makes such extensive use of numbers.

Every successful business needs to have at least one person who dedicates themselves to giving close attention to them. But that does not let everybody else off the hook. Anybody seeking to have an important role should have some understanding of which numbers matter and why. And for this they need to have some appreciation of balance sheets, profit and loss accounts and the rest. Fortunately, modern computers make easy work of compiling and organising the relevant figures. They even do some of the analysis. But individuals still need to know what such charts are telling them – and what this data means.

A balance sheet – like the accounts in general – is simply a snapshot of the state of the business at a certain moment. It shows the value of assets owned by the company and also who provided the funds with which to finance the assets and to whom the business is ultimately liable.

Assets are divided into fixed and current assets. The former group includes physical things, such as buildings and machinery; intangible assets, such as goodwill and intellectual property; and investments in other businesses. Current assets are cash, stock, works in progress and other things in the process of being turned into cash.

The funds used to buy the assets come from two main sources. They are provided by the owners through direct investment in the business or by allowing the business to retain some of the profits in reserve, or they are borrowed – from bankers or creditors. Together, these sources of funds are known as liabilities.

Borrowings are divided between creditors falling due within one year (overdrafts and the like) and creditors falling due after one year (usually longer-term loans at fixed rates of interest). Investors study balance sheets because they help them decide whether to back businesses through indicating the profitability of the business, whether its sales are seasonal, the strength of its reserves, the level of equity held by the owners and the like.

The diagram below shows that British balance sheets can be hard to read because all the information is set out vertically, with a figure for Working Capital (calculated by subtracting current liabilities from current assets) somewhat buried in the middle. This is in keeping with British accounting rules. But in the United States, assets and liabilities are laid out separately and horizontally, with the result that the balance sheet is easier to understand.

Obviously, this is a simplified version. Accounting for such things as Goodwill, the term used to describe the gap between an asset's (or a company's) market price and the price actually paid, and copyrights, designs and other forms of intellectual property requires complex rules relating to such concepts as amortisation and depreciation. Full descriptions of them can be found in the books referred to here and elsewhere.

The other important financial statement is the Profit and Loss Account, or – in the United States – the Income Statement. The P&L, as it is commonly known, is a

Sample Balance Sheet		
Assets	£000s	£000s
Current Assets		
Cash	5	
Owed by customers (debtors/receivables)	20	
Stocks (inventories)	0	
Total current assets		25
Fixed Assets		
Equipment		7
TOTAL ASSETS		32
Capital employed		
Owners' equity		
Share capital	28	
Retained earnings	4	
Total equity		32
CAPITAL EMPLOYED		32

summary of a business's income and expenses over an accounting period, usually a year. At its most basic, profit is the difference between income and expenses. But in practice there are different forms of profit.

Gross profit is what is left after all the costs relating to producing what you sell are taken from income. Operating profit is what is left when operating expenses are taken away from gross profit. Pre-tax profit (the figure usually quoted in news reports of company results) is what is left after deducting financing costs. Profit after tax is the amount that is available to be spent or reinvested in the business (net income). This is the "bottom line", as opposed to the "top line" represented by sales or revenues.

All these profit figures will be included in the P&L, along with the elements that go towards them. These are sales, plus any other revenues from operations; the cost of sales; operating expenses – selling and administration costs, depreciation, etc; non-operating revenues, such as rent and interest; non-operating expenses – financial and other costs not directly linked to the running of the business; and provision for tax.

Commentators and other business analysts tend to talk about pre-tax profits, because they represent the per-formance of the business after taking account of things over which the management has some control, such as operating costs and financing costs, without being affected by tax bills. However, in some circumstances they may prefer to look at other profit measures. For example, if the pre-tax profit is boosted by a one-off advantage, such as the sale of a business, it might be more useful to compare operating profits with those in the previous year.

FINANCIAL RATIOS

Comparing a company's balance sheets and profit and loss accounts from one year to the next is one way of assessing the financial health of a company. However, it only goes so far, and conclusions drawn from such analysis can be misleading.

Consequently, analysts of company accounts tend to make much use of ratios, or the relationships between pairs of figures taken from the accounts. Which pairs of figures are most relevant will obviously depend on what aspect of the accounts is of interest or what the analyst is seeking to discover. For example, it may in certain situations be useful to compare a ratio with its equivalent the previous year. In others it may be better to compare it with that of a competitor.

One of the most familiar ratios is the price earnings ratio, or PE, which is a measure of the value the stock market places on future earnings. It is the market price per share divided by the earnings per share, itself a ratio calculated by dividing net profit by the number of ordinary shares issued. Both these measures are widely-used stock-market measures of performance. Others are the yield – the percentage return a shareholder gains on the current value of his or her investment, which is calculated by dividing the dividends per share by the price per share- and the dividend cover – net income divided by the dividend and thus the number of times the profit exceeds the dividend (the share of profit in publicly-owned companies paid to shareholders). The higher the ratio the more funds there are available to be retained to invest in the business.

But there are many other ratios, all designed to give indications of the strength of different areas of performance.

For example, a common test of profitability is the profit margin, calculated by dividing the profit by sales, and multiplying by 100. Clearly, the higher the percentage the better, since higher margins are generally seen as good business. Which form of profit is used depends on what you are seeking to analyse. So, the gross profit margin measures the value the business adds to the materials and services bought in order to produce its good or service, while operating profit excludes financing costs and tax, which are generally outside the business's control. So the margin here will indicate how efficiently the operations of the business are being run (as opposed to how effective it is at managing financial issues, which would be measured by using profit before and after tax).

In addition, those interested in the solvency of the business will typically look at gearing – the proportion of all borrowing to the total funds. This gearing ratio is also known as the debt/equity ratio and should not generally exceed 1:1. Or they might consider the interest cover – a measure of the proportion of profit taken up by interest payments that is calculated by dividing the annual interest payments into the annual profit before interest, tax and dividend payments. The smaller the number the greater is the risk to the company from the level of borrowing.

FINANCE

Accounting is so closely related to finance that the two are often mixed up. After all, the person who is generally the most senior accountant in the business is the finance director or the chief financial officer. Roughly speaking, finance covers where the money to run a business comes from, while accounting – as you might expect – accounts for it. It is fair to assume that to understand one area you really need to understand the other.

Businesses can call upon many sources of funds. They bring different advantages and drawbacks, and will suit different businesses at different stages of their development. Managers with an appreciation of these differences will be better placed to choose between them should they have to.

Small businesses, from start-ups to even quite well-established businesses, tend to take a simple approach to finance, using retained profits, supplemented by bank loans of different types, when required. However, larger businesses – particularly those listed on stock markets – are more likely to have a variety of types of financing in place, ranging from share capital to various forms of loans.

Whatever the size of business, though, there are really only two sources of finance – equity and debt. Equity is simply capital supplied by the owner or owners. Such money is not a risk since it does not need to be repaid. Debt, on the other hand, is money borrowed by the business from outside sources. It is risky for the business because the lender can in certain circumstances ask for it back and because the interest payable on the loan is a cost irrespective of how the business is faring. It is also risky for the lenders – for them the interest rate is the reward they get for taking that risk, and they may charge a higher than usual rate if they feel the risk is high. As we have seen earlier, gearing is the term for the proportion of debt to equity and a ratio of 1:1 is preferred by bankers. However, some businesses deliberately opt for higher gearing levels if they see a chance to enhance the return on shareholder capital – with the risk that a fall in profits can leave them facing problems making their interest payments.

The most obvious source of debt is a bank. Businesses rely on banks to provide them with the money needed to run their operations. This is why the "credit crunch" that started in 2008 was so devastating for business. Banks suddenly faced with a shortfall in capital responded by equally suddenly cutting back on lending.

Assuming more normal business conditions, though, there are three main types of bank funding. They are Overdrafts, which are technically short-term loans since they can be called in whenever the bank wishes but tend to be a semi-permanent feature of many businesses' funding arrangements; Term Loans, or loans offered for set periods with interest charged at variable or fixed rates; and Government-backed Loans. These are provided by banks, usually to small businesses that have business plans that are deemed to be viable but cannot obtain regular loans, usually because they cannot offer the security required. These facilities are offered in such countries as Britain, the United States and Australia.

WHO SAID IT

"Rule Number One: Never Lose Money. Rule Number Two: Never Forget Rule Number One."
– Warren Buffett

One of the factors behind the credit crunch was the tendency for banks of all kinds to engage in increasingly complex lending arrangements (and in similarly complicated accounting procedures relating to them). This is not the place to go into them. However, it should be realised that there are other forms of borrowing – loosely grouped under mortgages, bonds and debentures. Business mortgages are much the same as those taken out by individuals. They are for a specific purpose, such as buying an office building, and the business has to pay interest with the lender securing the loan against the property so that the mortgage can be redeemed if the business falls into trouble. Businesses wanting to raise funds for general business purposes can raise money by issuing bonds or debentures. These run for a few years with the holders receiving interest over the life of the loan. Debentures and bonds are broadly similar except that debentures – because they are unsecured – carry greater risk for the holder. Traditionally, bonds and debentures were bought by investment institutions, but increasingly they are bought by individuals in much the same way as shares.

For growing businesses there are two other important sources of finance. The first is Leasing. Companies, often part of established banking groups, will lease anything a business needs – from cars to photocopiers – so that a business short of cash has the use of the items without having to pay for them outright. A variant is hire purchase, which differs in that the business has the option of buying the car or other item at the end of the agreement. The second source is the Factoring industry. Factoring involves providing a business that deals with other businesses rather than with private individuals a proportion of the money owed to it by customers in advance. This effective buying up of trade debts is particularly useful for businesses in the early stages of growth because they need the funds required to expand faster than their customers are paying them. A related concept is Invoice Discounting, which – as its name suggests – is also a means of a business obtaining cash against the value of its invoices but without losing control of its sales ledger. That is, it collects its own debts, but receives a loan against their value.

Equity capital comes in two broad forms – private equity and public capital. Private equity involves individuals (typically wealthy people often known as "business angels" rather than the "dragons" of TV fame) or groups (some of which are large international funds that rival investment banks in size and influence) providing funds in return for a share of the business. They usually invest because they see opportunities for greater returns than are likely in listed companies, but the risks are also correspondingly higher. Another type of private equity investment involves large companies investing in smaller ones, usually because they want early access to new developments. Such corporate venturing is common in the pharmaceutical industry and also in high-technology, where companies such as Microsoft and Cisco have billions of dollars invested in small entrepreneurial firms.

Public capital arises from a company issuing shares on a stock market. This process, which can raise anything from a few million to billions of pounds or dollars, essentially brings new owners into a business. In practice, because there are so many of them the owners are not involved (unless, like pension funds and other institutional investors, they hold so many shares that they have influence), but they do get to vote at the annual general meeting and on such matters as takeovers, and they receive any dividends paid. They may invest for the long term or sell their shares on to other investors. The share price quoted on the stock market reflects interest in the shares.

In addition to providing a means of obtaining the funds for expansion, a stock market listing also brings respectability. Without suggesting that private businesses are inferior, it is a fact that being a quoted company carries a status that creates a sort of virtuous circle by enabling the management to borrow more and so grow faster. Moreover, if the market likes a company its share price can rise sufficiently for it to be able to take over rivals without having to raise fresh finance. It can simply offer its shares in return for the target's.

Of course, listing on the stock market is not without its issues. First, it can just as easily become a victim of a takeover. Second, preparing for a listing (known as an intitial public offering, or IPO) can take a lot of management time and effort. Third, once on the market, the company's senior management then has to spend a lot of time keeping professional investors informed of its progress and ensuring it meets expectations.

It is for this last reason that many companies either stay private or opt to return to that status after a spell as a public company. However, being private does not always mean that the management is free of pressure. Private equity investors typically look to sell their investment after several years, so the management can find itself pressed just as much to perform.

TAX

Just as with individuals, tax is a weighty issue for businesses. In its various forms, tax can account for up to half of a business's turnover. Moreover, a tax bill is often the event that causes a struggling business to fail altogether. And should that happen, the tax authorities are also generally first in the line of creditors.

Tax regimes differ throughout the world but the principles are much the same. Essentially all but the smallest businesses – which as sole traders pay income tax – pay some form of corporation tax, the business equivalent of income tax. The amount tends to depend on the size of the business and on the amount of profit made. The picture is also clouded by allowances for such things as investment in plant and machinery and in research and development. However, such matters are constantly being altered depending on what governments are trying to encourage in the way of industry and how short of cash they are. Businesses are also liable for capital gains tax if they make a profit on the sale of assets and for business rates on their premises.

In addition to being responsible for calculating the amount of tax they owe, filing their computations with the tax authorities and paying the tax, they are responsible for collecting taxes on sales (value added tax, or VAT, in the EU) and for calculating and collecting the tax due from their employees. Because in many countries no two employees are alike as a result of the systems of allowances and tax credits, this can be a very complex procedure – even with the help of computing systems.

Unsurprisingly, given the amounts involved, businesses are generally keen to pay as little tax as possible. Public companies could even argue that they are obliged to take this approach. Again as with individuals, there is a thin line between tax avoidance, which is – under sufferance – permitted, and tax evasion, which is not. Some international companies go to great lengths to minimise their tax liabilities by organising themselves around the world in such a way that they make use of the lowest possible tax rates. However, the tax authorities in different countries are increasingly co-operating and cracking down on what they consider to be artificial arrangements. The financial crisis and the associated black holes in many countries' finances have only intensified moves in this direction. For example, Greece – traditionally a bastion of the "black economy" – has stepped up its attempts to encourage businesses as well as individuals to pay appropriate amounts of tax. At the same time, however, nations – aware that tax rates are a factor in businesses deciding where to locate – seek to compete with each other through claiming lower corporation tax rates.

Whatever happens, there is no denying that business is an important source of government revenue across the world. Governments in countries like Britain and the United States have in recent years generally sought to adopt a "hands-off" regulatory approach to banks and other financial institutions out of a recognition of their importance to wealth creation in general and tax revenues in particular.

It is all very well to have accounts neatly drawn up according to accounting rules and published at regular intervals. As we have seen, most of the elements in company accounts report on how things are at a particular time. This might be helpful for analysts looking at the past performance of a company but managers need information that is current and provides insights into future performance.

MANAGEMENT ACCOUNTING

Accordingly, a quite separate discipline – management accounting – has grown up to produce information that will help managers run the business, make decisions and plan for the future. Because management accounts are not required by law they can take many forms and be as detailed or as brief as the company concerned likes. They can also be produced as frequently as the needs of the business dictate. For instance, in a fast-moving industry like retail it is common for managers to have daily information on sales, stock levels and the like, while other businesses will be happy to have monthly reports.

Management accounts can also be used to track the performance of individual sites, divisions or products. This has become especially true since the arrival of cheap computing power enabled easy collection and dissemination of such data.

In addition, while financial accounts consciously do not record anything that cannot be given a monetary value, management accounts frequently include such non-financial data as customer transactions, numbers and productivity of employees and sales volumes.

Unsurprisingly, then, management accounting was in the vanguard of accepting the ideas behind the "balanced scorecard" and its related strategic management and measurement system, "activity-based costing". Harvard professor Robert Kaplan was involved in the development of both.

The balanced scorecard is explained in *The Balanced Scorecard: Translating Strategy into Action*, the book Kaplan wrote with David Norton, co-founder of the consulting company Renaissance Solutions. Essentially, the scorecard is designed to encourage managers away from their tendency to focus on a few measures and instead to gain an overall view by looking at a range of "key performance indicators".

WHO YOU NEED TO KNOW
Robert Kaplan

Robert Kaplan is a Harvard Business School professor who has worked extensively with David Norton, a consultant and founder of the firm Renaissance Solutions. The pair are famous for two concepts that have become commonplace in businesses – activity-based costing and the balanced scorecard. At the heart of their approach is measurement, particularly improving how corporate performance is measured. Norton is believed to have come up with the balanced scorecard approach after a game of golf. The business executive he had been playing with apparently remarked that what he needed to measure his business performance was a scorecard like that he had for a round of golf.

The two men's most famous book is *The Balanced Scorecard: Translating strategy into action* from 1996, but they have gone on to develop their approach and the idea that a firm's performance should be measured by more than financial measures has appealed to enthusiasts of sustainable business.

Some have likened the traditional reliance on financial measures in the accounts to driving while looking in the rear view mirror. Kaplan and Norton said that running a company was like flying a plane. Rather than relying on a single dial, which would be unsafe, pilots should make use of all the information available in their cockpits.

Furthermore, they argued that the increasing complexity of modern business made it essential that managers were able to check on performance in several areas at once. They also said that taking this approach would enable managers to see whether improvement in one area of the business came at the expense of another. Recent years have seen many computer software companies develop systems for collecting such data and analysing it quickly, so that many managers now have almost too much information.

It is worth remembering that Kaplan and Norton suggested that the balanced scorecard required four elements to be balanced. First is the "customer perspective". Companies need to ask how they are perceived by customers. Second is the "internal perspective". This means asking at what they must excel. Third is the "innovation and learning perspective", which means assessing whether they can continue to improve and so create value. Fourth is the "financial perspective", or how the business looks to shareholders.

Companies that focus on all of these elements become driven by their mission rather than short-term financial performance, claimed Kaplan and Norton.

Activity-based costing continues the focus on information. By allocating precisely direct and indirect costs to particular products or customer segments, ABC aims to provide a realistic means of calculating the true cost of doing business. As *The Financial Times Handbook of Management* points out, the concept is in some ways a financial version of re-engineering, or business process re-engineering, the management idea that swept business in the 1990s and involved companies identifying their key processes and making them as lean and as efficient as possible.

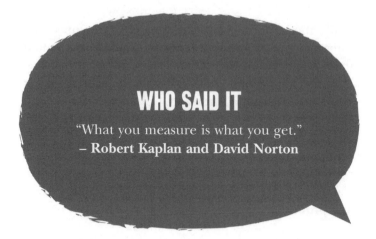

WHO SAID IT

"What you measure is what you get."
– **Robert Kaplan and David Norton**

Made popular by James Champy, co-founder of the consultancy CSC Index, and Michael Hammer, a former MIT computer science professor, in their book *Re-engineering the Corporation*, re-engineering was touted as a "manifesto for business revolution". But it could be argued that it was really a follow-on from such ideas as scientific management and total quality management. Having said that, it spawned many other books as well as a few management consultancies dedicated to re-engineering and played an important role in giving companies the tools for cutting bureaucracy and wastage in their operations. Like ABC, it requires managers to look carefully at what they do and why.

TRIPLE BOTTOM LINE

While the balanced scorecard and ABC are concerned with giving those inside the business more information than comes from traditional accounting, the Triple Bottom Line is more about answering outside concerns about how a business runs itself. Coined in 1994 by John Elkington, the pioneering sustainability consultant, the term refers to the practice of expanding the traditional reporting framework to take into account social and environmental measures in addition to the traditional financial measures. The three bottom lines are people, planet and profits.

The British telecommunications company BT and the Anglo-Dutch oil company Shell were among the first companies to start publishing environmental and social reports in addition to their usual reports and accounts. Then, the practice became widespread as the notion of Corporate Social Responsibility took hold.

This is a rapidly-developing concept that has seen a variety of businesses become increasingly involved in areas that were previously regarded as the preserve of government and/or charities. At the same time, executives are increasingly seeing the business case for such activities on the basis that all businesses need thriving communities in which to prosper. Moreover, being environmentally responsible can actually boost profitability through discouraging waste. So there is a financial aspect to this information, which is also likely to be of interest to the readers of traditional financial accounts.

Indeed, with governments requiring more attention to sustainability and even in some cases requiring that companies pay attention to their wider role in society, approaches such as the Triple Bottom Line that were regarded as revolutionary only a short while ago are increasingly mainstream.

WHAT YOU NEED TO READ

▶ A good starting point for understanding the significance of business numbers is Michael Brett's *How To Read the Financial Pages* (Random House). Similar approaches are offered in *The Sunday Times: How To Understand Business Finance* (Kogan Page) by Robert

Cinnamon, Brian Helweg-Larsen and Paul Cinnamon and *The Times: How The City Really Works* (Kogan Page) by Alexander Davidson.

▶ The *Financial Times Handbook of Management* (FT/Prentice Hall) and *A Student's Guide to Auditing* by Alan Lewin and *A Student's Guide to Analysing Corporate Reports* by Paul Robins (both Kaplan Publishing) are all helpful.

▶ Terry Smith's *Accounting For Growth* (Random House) helped bring to light some of the most notorious accounting tricks of the late twentieth century, while *Cannibals With Forks: The Triple Bottom Line of 21st Century Business* (Capstone) is John Elkington's pioneering work on the "triple bottom line".

IF YOU ONLY REMEMBER ONE THING

Finance is the money that funds a business, accounting is the way people keep a record of the money in a business. Profit is key, but cashflow will ultimately determine whether a business survives or fails.

CHAPTER 5

THE STRATEGY

WHAT IT'S ALL ABOUT

▶ **What Strategy Is**

▶ **How To Get a Strategy**

▶ **Business Plans and Forecasts**

▶ **Strategy Trends**

Few things are talked about in business circles with such passion as strategy. Read the business press and the columns are peppered with such statements as "Company X set out its strategy as …", "Y resigned because his strategy had not produced results" and "Z said the company's success was down to a clear strategy of …"

So what is this thing called strategy? Like many concepts in business, it is derived from the military. It is derived from the Greek word "strategos", which is roughly translated as general. In the armed services, strategy is the branch that deals with the planning and conduct of war. And so it pretty much is in business. A strategy is a plan of action devised with the aim of achieving a particular goal. It can be distinguished from tactics, which involves merely responding to events, through being generally elaborate and systematic.

DEVISING A STRATEGY

When a new business is set up it will – if it wants to win financial backing – have to set out at least a basic strategy. Typically, the founders will have seen a gap in the market and will devise a means of filling it (the strategy). Accordingly, when Ocado, the British online grocer, started in partnership with the upscale supermarket chain Waitrose in 2002 it was determined to revolutionise online grocery shopping. The concept, introduced on the back of the internet – but, of course, something of a throwback to the old days of having goods delivered by the local grocer's lad on his bike – was, it has to be said, suffering from an image problem stemming from delivery times not always being met and what was arriving at the door often not matching exactly what was ordered. As a result, shoppers did not feel as if they could rely on the services and still had to do what they were presumably trying to avoid – go shopping. The founders of Ocado saw an opportunity, based around quality and service. As the company website states: "Ocado was conceived with one simple objective in mind: to offer busy people a true alternative to going to the supermarket every week. And in doing so, we created a totally new shopping experience, built entirely around their needs." As the company develops, it adds features, but the basic premise remains the same.

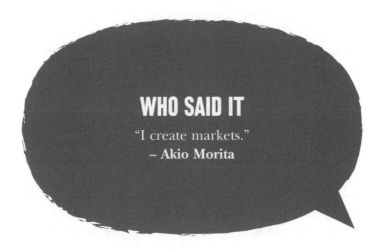

WHO SAID IT

"I create markets."
– **Akio Morita**

At other times – and this is probably the most common situation – a new strategy is introduced. It may follow a change of leadership. New chief executives are very fond of marking their arrival with big changes. Or it may follow a major setback for the company or just a period when the company has fallen back in relation to its competitors. Often, such a change will follow the new leadership introducing to the business a team of management consultants (of which more later) who will analyse what the business does, how it does it and then generally offer an opinion of what it should be doing.

Some strategies are brutally simple. Many years ago, the Japanese heavy machinery maker Komatsu launched a fightback against its US arch-rival under the rallying cry "Encircle Caterpillar". Others are rather more complex and have contributed to the rise of "mission statements" as executives have sought to boil down their essence so that they can be easily understood.

So a strategy does not have to be set in stone. Indeed, in recent years events have been happening so fast that it could be seen as foolish to stick to anything like a five-year plan. However, you do need to have some sort of idea of what the business is trying to do and how, even if you do adapt as you go along. This is particularly important if the company is trying to encourage employees to embark on something challenging or they are required to change their behaviour. Moreover, at a time when both the business environment and the nature of the business a company is in are so complex it could be argued that it is more important than ever that there be a clear focus.

STUMBLING UPON SUCCESS

It is true that some companies stumble upon success. They may start in one area or be using one approach and then realise that a different segment of the market or a different approach is more likely to work for them.

For example, Rackspace Hosting, which has been one of the leaders in the development of "cloud computing", or using the internet to outsource storage of data and other functions, attributes much of its success to the delivery of a unique form of customer service that they call "Fanatical Support". But as founding investor Graham Weston relates, that was not always the case. Originally believing that they were simply offering a cut-price product, he and his colleagues did not see the need for service. But then they realised that if you were asking somebody to trust you with an important part of their business, you must hire helpful experts who would answer the phone, and who could solve their customers' problems. Of course, Rackspace could have offered a level of service that they thought reflected the cost of what they were providing. Instead, they decided to go to the extreme and launched "fanatical support". It is a powerful market differentiator that has won the company lots of awards along the way and, more important, enabled a little business from San Antonio, Texas, to compete with the likes of Amazon, IBM and Oracle and grow to annual sales of $ 700m in 2010. Rackspace learned that listening to your customers and giving them what they want – even if it's not what you originally wanted to deliver – can be a very powerful strategy.

THE BUSINESS PLAN

The most basic means of giving focus to the business and particularly to its employees is the business plan. This is what the bank manager or any other would-be financier would be looking for before backing an entrepreneur's business. Various websites, books and different bodies offer advice on preparing business plans, which can be a daunting prospect for people seeking to start their first enterprise.

However, there really isn't a lot of mystery to it. Essentially, it includes a summary of what the business does or is setting out to do, how it started and where the founder and/or current management want it to go. Experts point out that there is a particular need to cover the strategy for improving sales and processes in order to achieve the targets that have been set. Business plans typically cover periods of one or two years.

As for the specifics, the sound business plan should set out the Marketing aims and objectives. For example, the

WHO SAID IT

"Strategies are intellectually simple;
their execution is not."
– **Larry Bossidy**

business might describe what the customer base is likely to look like at the end of the period covered. It should also include Operational information – such as, say, where the business is based, who and where the suppliers are and the sort of investment required for premises and equipment. Naturally, financial information – such as profit and loss accounts, cashflow and sales forecasts and, if the business has already been operating for some time, audited accounts – should also be included.

Strategy – on one level, at least – involves deciding on and setting out pretty much a grown-up version of this, with the sophistication dependent on the size and complexity of the business. The issue is not so much the writing of the strategy but deciding which approach to adopt. This can be especially fraught since nothing goes in and out of fashion quite like a strategy theory.

STRATEGY – A SHORT HISTORY

There is some dispute as to how long strategy has been around as a business discipline. Various elements were put in place in the early years of the twentieth century, when business started to become bigger and more organised. But it is generally reckoned that it came of age in the period between the beginning of the 1960s and the mid-1970s.

In this time, academics began to devote more time to the study of strategy. At the forefront were Theodore Levitt, the Harvard Business School marketing guru who was among the first to urge businesses to focus on customers rather than products, and H. Igor Ansoff, whose *Corporate Strategy* was hugely influential in developing strategic planning and helped pave the way for diversification.

However, the real developments took place outside the classroom. As Richard Koch, a successful entrepreneur and author of many books on strategy, says in *The Financial Times Guide to Strategy*, "perhaps the most important development in the history of strategy was the founding in 1964 of the Boston Consulting Group". By the end of the decade, adds Koch (a former BCG consultant), founder Bruce Henderson "had built a powerful machine combining intellectual innovation and boardroom consulting, and had invented both the Experience Curve and the Growth/Share Matrix, probably the two most powerful tools in the history of strategy."

THE EXPERIENCE CURVE

Originally the "learning curve", the Experience Curve represents the view that when the total number ("accumulated production") of any good or service doubles, unit costs when adjusted for inflation have the potential to fall by 20 to 30%. It is not connected to time, since in a very fast-growing product the doubling of production can occur in months, while for slower-growth products it can take years.

BCG's theory is based on many instances the firm discovered in the late 1960s and 1970s when accumulated production increased rapidly and inflation-adjusted costs fell 70 to 80%. One of the most important examples was the fall in the cost of integrated circuits, which explained the steep fall in the price of calculators.

BCG used the experience tool to identify cost reduction opportunities and also to describe and influence the battle between competitors in particular markets. The firm went on to develop a variant that related to prices rather than costs. This was particularly effective in showing how market leaders should reduce prices at least as fast as costs in order to keep competitors out and consolidate the market-leading position. BCG claimed that such thinking – even if, as some commentators believe, it did not involve the actual drawing of curves – explained how, for example, Honda was able to succeed so spectacularly in the motorcycle industry.

Although there are elements of the approach in the quality movement that swept the corporate world in the 1980s and the business process re-engineering wave that followed it, Koch says experience curve thinking has fallen out of favour in western companies – even though it "should be an integral part of good management".

The Boston Matrix

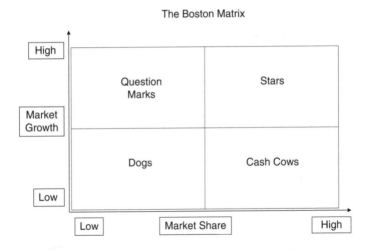

THE GROWTH/SHARE MATRIX

BCG invented several matrices, giving rise to what is arguably the management consultant's most familiar presentational tool – the two-by-two box. This one – sometimes called the BCG Matrix – is the most famous. It was invented in the 1960s and remains highly relevant. It measures market growth and relative market share for all the business a particular company has.

Adherents stress the necessity of precision in the terms used in the technique, particularly the definition of the two axes in the matrix. The horizontal axis – relative market share – means the share of the market the business has relative to the share held by its largest competitor. Say company A has a 40% share in business Y and its nearest competitor has a 10% share. In this case, company A's relative market share is 400%, or four times. In business X, company A may only have a 5% share and the leading competitor 10%. In this case, company A's relative market share is 50%. The vertical axis represents the growth rate of the market in which the business competes. Although there is some confusion about the precise definition of this market growth rate, the correct one is expected future annual growth rate in volume of the market as a whole. That is, not the expected growth rate of the individual company.

The real business of the matrix, though, and the element that has given rise to such staples of the business language as "cash cows" and "dogs", lies in the four quadrants of the matrix.

The bottom left box contains the Cash Cows (sometimes known as gold mines). Such businesses have high relative market share and ought to be profitable. They are very valuable and should be protected at all costs. They also produce a lot of cash, which can be reinvested in the business or elsewhere in the portfolio, used to buy other businesses or paid out to shareholders.

The top left box has the Stars, which are businesses that have high relative market share and are in high-growth markets. They are highly profitable but may need a lot of cash in order to maintain their position. Management should do and/or spend whatever it takes to hold or gain market share in such businesses. If relative market share is held, they will become cash cows when market growth slows; if it is not they will end up as Dogs.

The top right box holds Question Marks, or Wildcats. They have low relative market share but are in high-growth markets. Businesses in this quadrant are called question marks because their future is uncertain and the decision whether to invest in the business is both important and difficult. If a business does not improve its relative market share it, too, will become a dog. If it does it can become a star and then a cash cow. The problem is that it is not always clear what will happen even if management decides to invest in order to improve market share. Many question mark businesses – like, says Koch, much of the British computer industry – turn into Cash Traps. That is money is put in a business that never becomes a market leader, making the money a waste rather than an investment.

The final box belongs to the dogs – businesses with low relative market share in low-growth businesses. This looks desperate, especially since many of a company's businesses may be in this group. However, commentators point out that this may not be true. Although companies should beware of investing too much in dog businesses, dogs can become cash cows by perhaps resegmenting the business or by competing with the market leader on customer service. Even a modest amount of investment or adjustment of the business might improve its market share.

As with any theory or technique, there are weaknesses. For example, high market share is not the only thing that makes businesses successful and growth is not the only indicator of the attractiveness of a market. But the Matrix has stood the test of time because it encourages managers to analyse their businesses and because it exposes one of the failings of companies' strategies – taking a "one size fits all" approach, with the result that one type of business may have too little investment and another not enough.

In addition, the Matrix has been influential in inspiring variants – both within BCG and outside the firm. For example, the American industrial giant GE and McKinsey developed the GE/McKinsey Matrix as a means of planning the portfolio management approach for which GE became so famed. It built on the BCG grid by making the vertical axis Market Attractiveness rather than Market Growth and the horizontal axis Competitive Strength rather than Market Share and it added sophistication by making the grid 3x3 rather than 2x2. Such analysis was at the heart of GE's policy under Jack Welch of wanting to only be in markets in which it was a leader. Another management consultancy, Arthur D. Little, developed a rather complicated version centred on product life cycle as the key factor.

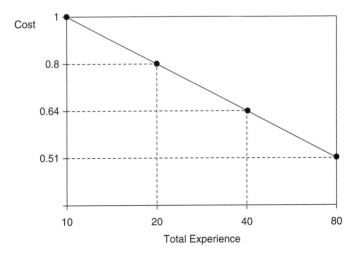

In effect, what BCG did was to link market analysis and research with financial theory to produce the micro-economic analysis of businesses and their competitors that became the heart of strategy as practised by other such well-known and influential firms as Bain & Co and McKinsey & Co. Because these analyses – often produced by bright young graduates – were so compelling, the consultants soon gained great influence in boardrooms across the world. With companies of all shapes and sizes increasingly desperate for advice and insights, the ranks of these consultancies and the many others that grew up in their wake swelled exponentially.

Strategy was suddenly the game everybody wanted to play and those who had played it – if even for a comparatively short while – greatly enhanced their employability in all areas of commerce and – as business began to become all-pervasive – increasingly in public life, too.

RISE OF McKINSEY

If the 1960s and early 1970s were dominated by BCG, it could be argued that the 1980s belonged to McKinsey. Started in the 1920s as a practice specialising in budgeting and finance, it moved into what is now known as consulting after founder James O. McKinsey decided to test his theory that "management engineers" could not just rescue sick companies but help healthy ones thrive and grow. For the next half century, McKinsey grew alongside the businesses it advised, to the extent of being in the vanguard of US corporations' expansion overseas. This mirroring of its clients' experience continued in the 1970s oil shock caused by troubles in the Middle east led to a period of deep recession. But in the 1980s it emerged as a real force, with many of its consultants vying with business school academics as major influences on the way business was conducted.

Key among these were Tom Peters and Robert Waterman, whose *In Search of Excellence* has good claim to be the best-known management book ever. Building on the codifying of knowledge and techniques that McKinsey had embarked upon in the 1970s, the book is widely seen as an attempt to boost the ego of corporate America, which was taking a battering from the rise of Japanese companies, such as Honda, Toyota and Sony, through giving examples of home-grown excellence. Unfortunately, within a few years of the book's publication, many of these companies started to look less great. Yet the book has still gone on to sell millions of copies and Peters used it as the launchpad for a career that saw him become the management consulting industry's leading guru, packing out lecture halls for talks notable for their religious-type fervour.

Although the examples in the book have not stood the test of time, the ideas in it – notably the need for passion, leadership, values and a focus on the customer – have. And, while some decry Peters's messianic style and the slightness of some of his later works, he has certainly been inspirational. After a period when business seemed to be largely about sitting in a cubicle poring over spreadsheets, he made it seem fun and exciting. In short, a place where passionate people with a will to make things happen should be. As such, his influence can be seen in the rush of start-ups in the internet boom and in the continuing enthusiasm for entrepreneurialism.

Peters and Waterman (who became more studious and introspective in his writings while Peters became a star) might have been the most prominent, but they were not the only people associated with McKinsey to make their mark on the strategy arena.

WHO YOU NEED TO KNOW
Tom Peters

Even before he helped change the world of management thinking with *In Search of Excellence*, the book he co-authored with Robert Waterman, Tom Peters had enjoyed a high-flying career. He studied engineering at Cornell University, served in Vietnam, worked for the US Government's Drug Enforcement Agency and had a PhD and an MBA from Stanford before joining the management consultancy McKinsey & Co.

Excellence was a major factor in the explosion in the management book market and Peters became a hugely successful speaker, to the extent that his stirring lectures probably eclipsed his future books. The first book was largely based on the large companies he and his fellow consultant came across in their work, but he later moved on to extol the virtues of entrepreneurial organisations. Indeed, Peters' lasting influence is arguably that he has urged all businesses to be passionate about what they are doing. But he was also one of the first to spot that the world was becoming more complex and chaotic. Peters has played a key part in urging businesses to constantly re-examine themselves.

For example, Kenichi Ohmae, who ran the firm's Japanese operation for many years, explained in his 1982 book *The Mind of the Strategist* how Japanese companies had secured an advantage over their US rivals through their leaders – who often had little of the formal business education of their American counterparts – using vision and intuition to turn their ideas into action. Later books, such as *The Borderless World*, helped to explain the rise of globalisation and its effects. In addition, the firm's journal, *The McKinsey Quarterly* became as eagerly read as the *Harvard Business Review* for those looking for the new trends in business and ways of addressing fresh challenges.

COMPETITIVE STRATEGY

The 1980s also saw the arrival of the hugely influential Michael Porter. Another Harvard academic, Porter has effectively changed the way that business people think about competition through applying to strategy the language and concepts of economics.

While competitive advantage and clustering help to explain the success of certain companies' and countries' strategies, it is the value-chain concept that has arguably led to changes in how businesses organise themselves. Other writers have developed the value-chain concept in various ways, including the idea that business is a series of processes. But it was Porter who introduced the notion that each link of the chain added value (another term much used in recent years that basically means something that a customer is prepared to pay for) so that even support activities – such as how the company trained its people or paid them – had value and were therefore sources of competitive advantage. His point was that businesses in the same industry might have to do the same things, but that they do them differently – a difference that could be a source of competitive advantage. Porter cited how People Express, a pioneer in low-cost aviation, was essentially in the same business as the more traditional carrier United Airlines, but gained a competitive advantage through its approach to such matters as running the boarding gate and organising crews.

WHO YOU NEED TO KNOW
Michael Porter

Michael Porter became one of Harvard's youngest ever tenured professors when he joined the school's faculty at the age of 26. And he has certainly not disappointed. His books *Competitive Strategy* and *Competitive Advantage* echo the comparative advantage thinking of the nineteenth century economist David Ricardo to provide a framework for companies seeking to outpace their rivals. This comes down to Porter's belief that companies can, in the words of management writer Tim Hindle, "win either by being cheaper or by being different (which means being perceived by the customer as better or more relevant)." Not as well known as other management gurus – his books are deliberately academic in tone and as such are hardly bestsellers – Porter has nevertheless probably been more influential than all of them. Thanks to him, "competitive advantage" is part of the business lexicon and he was also responsible for identifying the concept of clustering – the explanation for why even in an era of easy communications like-minded

businesses locate near each other, whether
they are Hollywood film studios and related
businesses, internet companies in Silicon
Valley and other hotspots or even bulb growers
in the Netherlands – and the idea that a
firm is a series of activities linked together
in a "value chain".

CORE COMPETENCES

Among the key advances in strategy thinking since
Porter has been the notion of Core Competences
introduced by Gary Hamel and C.K. Prahalad and an
alternative approach to running portfolios of businesses
based on the idea that the central organisation acts as a
sort of "parent".

Hamel, an American associated with the London Business
School, and Prahalad, an Indian and his sometime

colleague at the University of Michigan, originally impressed the business world with an article on "strategic intent", but they really made their names in 1990 with the *Harvard Business Review* article "The Core Competence of the Corporation", one of the magazine's best-selling reprints ever.

They identified core competences as "the collective learning in the organisation, especially how to co-ordinate diverse production skills and integrate multiple streams of technologies". In addition, they distinguished these intangible assets from their physical counterparts on the grounds that, rather than deteriorating over time, they were "enhanced" as they were applied and shared.

As such, the approach became tied up in the enthusiasm for knowledge management that gripped the 1990s business world as companies increasingly realised – in keeping with the principles of Porter's value chain – that it was not just what you did but how you did it that mattered in the increasingly competitive world. This was also the time when companies really began to see their workers not as costs nor even as their greatest assets but as "human capital" with a value to match that of their brands and other intangibles.

OUTSOURCING

Perhaps even more importantly, the idea of core competences helped to underpin the trend against diversification (the industrial conglomerate Hanson was one of many such entities to split itself into its component parts in the 1990s) and in favour of outsourcing.

It could be argued that outsourcing has been around for ever in that, for example, advertising companies have handled companies' marketing for years, while certain financial activities have long been handled by specialists. But it really took off as a concept in the 1990s after Andersen Consulting (now Accenture) took over the day-to-day accounting operations of the oil company BP, a move that was swiftly followed by other companies and other technology-based consulting firms. The rationale was that firms such as Andersen could do the work better and more cheaply because it was what they concentrated on. In other words, this was their core competence. Meanwhile, BP could focus (another watchword of the years since the 1990s) on its core activities of exploring for oil, drilling it, refining it, etc.

The problem was that in an increasingly complex and competitive world in which new specialist businesses using ever-developing technology are appearing constantly it can be difficult to distinguish core and non-core activities.

Hamel and Prahalad have attempted to deal with that issue with a three-part test. A core competence provides potential access to a wide variety of markets, it makes a significant contribution to the perceived customer benefits of the end product and it is difficult for competitors to imitate because it is a complex combination of individual technologies and production skills. In short, core competences are those things that a business does exceptionally well.

This might sound vague enough compared with the plans and frameworks that characterised the early days of strategy. But it helped pave the way for a more fluid, opportunistic approach. Indeed, leaders of large corporations are increasingly urged to be more agile and to ape entrepreneurs in watching for signs of where the next opportunities might be – all the while keeping the business lean (again like an entrepreneurial business) and in a position to grow and so add value.

Even the proponents of a theory for managing portfolio businesses – Michael Goold, Andrew Campbell and Marcus Alexander of Britain's Ashridge Strategic Management Centre – put "creating value" in the subtitle of the book in which they set out their ideas. *Corporate-Level Strategy*, which appeared in 1994 with, incidentally, words of approval from Hamel, was an attempt to identify a "valid role for the parent organisation" at a time when many companies were under pressure to break themselves up into their component parts.

The reason for this was a perception that many conglomerates destroyed rather than created value. This terminology, which took hold in the 1990s, refers to the idea that the central organisation was an impediment to the development of the company rather than an aid.

Campbell (ex-McKinsey), Goold (ex-BCG) and Alexander (ex-BCG) decided that there were essentially three different parenting styles – strategic planning, strategic control and financial control. Each of these styles was suitable in certain types of business and unsuitable in others and companies had to decide whether businesses under their control fitted whichever of these styles they exhibited. If not, they should be sold off or otherwise divested.

The diversification/focus argument is never really settled. Each approach has its adherents and many companies shift between them depending on the circumstances in the economy generally and their markets in particular.

The auto industry is a case in point. The German luxury car maker BMW is often lauded for becoming highly profitable by sticking essentially to making just a few models united by the fact that they were stylish, sporty and expensive. Mercedes, in contrast, offers a huge variety of models, with some ranges only subtly different from others, with the result that its portfolio is seen as being difficult to manage. Moreover, its (since dissolved) merger with Chrysler of the United States was felt to have weakened its position as a luxury marque. However, it could argue that its economies of scale and ability to offer the Mercedes experience to many different types of customer made for a better long-term bet.

Ford took a similar approach – albeit from the opposite direction. It sought to move out of the commodity business of supplying reasonably stylish vehicles for "everyman" by building a "prestige" division around Volvo, Jaguar and Land Rover. But the plan soon foundered, with all three marques being sold almost before the operation got going.

Diversification is generally defended as offering protection against being too dependent upon one market. However, it can be risky in that the company may not have experience of the new products or services it is offering or of the markets it is seeking to enter.

The concept its generally seen as having four categories, each with their own risks. Horizontal diversification involves offering new products in the company's current market; vertical diversification is what happens if a company moves either backwards into a supplier's business or forwards into a customer's; concentric diversification is the introduction of a new product closely related to existing ones into a new market; and conglomerate diversification is introducing a completely new product into a new market.

Commonly, companies seek to reduce this risk by merging or taking over another company. Deals like this happen in each category. Sometimes, they are defensive, such as when well-established large steel companies join together in the hope of fending off competition from a new and vigorous new entrant through cutting costs and gaining from economies of scale. At other times, they are motivated by a desire to gain a presence in a market more quickly than would be possible through organic growth.

This is often the case in the technology and pharmaceuticals industries, where large companies hope to gain an advantage through having access to new developments, while the new entrants win access to the greater scale enjoyed by the large players in such as finance and marketing.

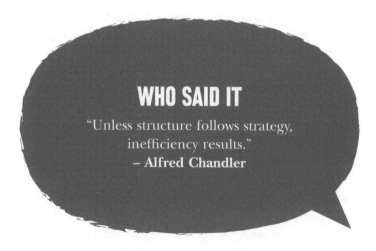

WHO SAID IT

"Unless structure follows strategy, inefficiency results."
– Alfred Chandler

So, companies still talk about having the "right strategy" or a "strategy for growth", etc. But increasingly – whether they are tiny start-ups or large groups – they are likely to be much more pragmatic about it than were their predecessors half a century ago. Strategy has – through the work of the people cited above (and the adaptations of others) – evolved into more of an attitude of mind rather than a set ambition or intent.

The internet and other technological developments enable businesses to operate in ways totally different to what was the case even a few years ago – with virtual teams spread around the globe, back-office functions out-sourced to one locality, design and manufacturing to others. Some will have core values holding them together, others will be more fluid. It is not easy to see which models will succeed in the future. Certainly, past attempts by experts (*In Search of Excellence*, James C. Collins and Jerry I. Porras's *Built To Last*, etc) have not been entirely successful.

It could be that the size or shape of the organisation is not as important as the general approach of the management or its attention to one or more particular facets. For example, take the technology world. Some concentrate on just one area, such as Apple with its iPad and iPod and other portable devices. On the other hand, Amazon started as an online book retailer but always saw itself simply as a technology company and has moved into selling books, CDs, DVDs, shoes and electrical goods and has also produced its own electronic reading device, the Kindle. Who can say which is right? Events – as in politics – are important in determining whether a venture succeeds. But so, too, are people. It is one thing to come up with a good or even brilliant strategy. It is quite another to implement it. That requires commitment, a clear sense of what the business is trying to do and people with the skills and intuition to do it.

WHAT YOU NEED TO READ

▶ There are too many books on strategy to give them all due credit. Some of the key texts are referred to above and others are described in such books as *Business, The Ultimate Resource* (A&C Black) and the *Financial Times Handbook of Management* (FT/Prentice Hall). Tim Hindle's *The Economist Guide to Management Ideas and Gurus* (Profile Books) is also useful, while Richard Koch's *Financial Times Guide to Strategy* (FT/Prentice Hall) shows how the discipline has developed. The work of one of the most influential firms is described in *Perspectives on Strategy: From the Boston Consulting Group* (John Wiley & Sons), edited by Carl W. Stern and George Stalk Jr.

▶ Colin Barrow also offers the benefit of his experience as a business person and an academic in *The 30 Day MBA* (Kogan Page).

IF YOU ONLY REMEMBER ONE THING

Strategy is how businesses define their
ambitions. In recent years strategy has evolved
into more of a state of mind than a clear
set of goals.

CHAPTER 6

THE FUNCTIONS

WHAT IT'S ALL ABOUT

- ▶ How Business is Organised
- ▶ How the Different Functions Work
- ▶ Sales and Marketing
- ▶ Operations
- ▶ Information Technology
- ▶ Human Resources
- ▶ Communications

In a small business it is generally obvious who runs the show. Everybody reports to him or her. Moreover, in the smallest businesses the team will inevitably be small, with many members carrying out more than one role. Specialisation comes as the business grows. Accordingly, employees will be split into different groups, each doing a certain type of work, but reporting to particular executives, either on the board or below it.

It is important that how this works is clear to everybody involved. This is why companies typically have organisational charts showing who reports to whom. However, there are various different ways in which organisations can structure themselves and their organisational charts will reflect that.

The basic organisational structure has every member or part of the organisation reporting to a single person. This basic structure can be based on functions, such as marketing or manufacturing; geography, such as country or region; product; and customer or market segment, i.e. trade, consumers or key accounts.

It is generally reckoned that the fewer people a manager has reporting to him or her the better. This is because the larger the number (or the wider the span of control) the more difficult communication and control become. The problem is that as the organisation becomes bigger the narrow span of control approach requires more layers of management – making the organisation more bureaucratic and, it is assumed, less able to respond to changes in the market.

Basic Organisational Chart

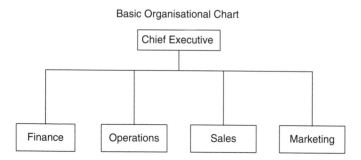

On the other hand, the flat management structure associated with a wide span of control involves fewer management layers but requires rather more of each manager. This is because they will typically be performing a wider range of tasks. The ability of the organisation to deal with this will depend on such factors as the ability of the managers as a whole, the skill levels of those being managed and the nature of the business (if the manager is responsible for a set of largely identical units and is supported by good control systems he or she may be able to deal with it better than if the business has a range of operations). Accordingly, a manager of a highly-skilled workforce operating in a business split into broadly similar units can deal with rather more staff than a counterpart in charge of a team in need of a lot of supervision working in varying areas.

Typically, in small and medium-sized businesses managers start out performing many roles themselves –

including hiring and firing, accounts keeping and perhaps marketing. But as the company gets bigger it makes more sense to create teams of specialists, or functions, to support general managers. This can create confusion over responsibilities, but generally the specialists advise on their areas of expertise and the line manager takes ultimate responsibility.

Sometimes, a business may become big enough that it can divide itself into what are effectively separate businesses. These strategic business units are responsible for their own profit or loss and have a great deal of autonomy, but are answerable to the top management.

However, other big businesses opt for what is known as a matrix organisation. This is an attempt to improve management accountability by effectively giving an individual or unit two bosses. It is most often associated with multinationals, where a business unit will report to a country head and a global function, such as marketing or finance. But it can also be used in other businesses, such as those built around projects, where members of staff report into a practice area and also to the project itself.

Mark Lancelott, a human resources and change management expert at PA Consulting Group, says:

> "Giving individuals a secondary reporting line can seem easy – just add a dotted line on the organisation chart – but it is difficult in practice. How do

you make sure your dotted lines aren't broken lines: that is, that there is a true management relationship? And if they are broken, what can you do to fix them?

These questions are not easy to answer. It's not surprising that we often see matrix relationships that aren't working effectively, whether it's business partner teams working to their customers' agenda – to the detriment of corporate policy – or operational units building their own capability rather than taking advantage of the matrix function to access and share corporate resources."

Partly because of the complexity involved and the potential rivalries, especially in multinational businesses, and also because there has been a general movement away from a general top-down directive type of management towards one based around empowered teams, the approach has fallen in popularity. It has either been dropped or adapted in line with the growing enthusiasm for working in multi-function teams and projects. This "new matrix management" involves groups collaborating to get particular projects done or to serve particular customers and then drawing on specialist support from the different functions within the company.

In days gone by, individuals would typically spend their whole careers working in one area of the business. Increasingly, though, businesses have sought to abandon this "silo" approach and encourage people to move around functions, picking up knowledge and experience and making the contacts that can assist with a more collaborative style of working. As a result, anybody in business should have some knowledge of the different parts that go together to make a successful business work. Consequently, the rest of this chapter will provide an introduction to each of the main functions – sales and marketing, operations, information technology, human resources and communications. You will learn what they do and how and also have an idea of how they contribute to the success of the business as a whole.

SALES AND MARKETING

A business can have developed the greatest product or service there has ever been, but if it does not sell the business will not succeed. This is why some of the most successful entrepreneurs are great sales people. Through a mixture of self-belief, a way with words and a bond with people, they are able to convince investors to back them and potential customers to buy from them.

It is one thing, however, to sell something once, quite another to keep selling it. Equally, the challenges of encouraging people to buy something new are quite different from those associated with getting them to choose your product or service from a crowded field. In some cases, the new product or service will appeal just because it is new. It is fresh and makes the buyer feel good for being at the "cutting edge". On the other hand, customers can be unwilling to try new things, either because they are happy enough to carry on using something that they feel does the job and appears to be reasonably priced or because they are simply suspicious of the new and want others to try it first.

A lot will depend on the product or service and who it is being sold to. For example, clients buying legal services are likely to put reliability and proven track record over innovation, while those seeking a new information technology system might value one that is more advanced than that of rivals and so could give the buyer a competitive advantage. Similarly, selling washing powder requires a different approach from selling an electronic gadget.

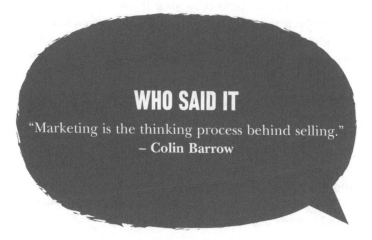

WHO SAID IT

"Marketing is the thinking process behind selling."
– Colin Barrow

Sales and marketing tend to be grouped together, though it is fair to say that people tend to prefer to think they are in marketing rather than sales. This is because it is perceived as being more strategic. It is the process of finding the right people to buy a product or service and making them aware that the business can meet their needs at a competitive price.

That said, there is a lot of technique and some science involved in selling. Marketing will get a business so far, but getting people to actually sign on the dotted line or hand over their cash requires something else – selling.

Although some people believe that sales people are born rather than made, selling can in fact be learned and improved like most other aspects of business. The basics of selling are that it is a process that at its most effective involves the sales person moving from the stage where he or she listens to the needs of the customer, through demonstrating how they can meet these needs and answering questions to "closing the sale". Good sales people also plan and keep records so that they know when would-be customers might be ready to buy or to reorder, such as when their car insurance runs out.

So much for the end-game. Unless they are relying on old-fashioned "cold-calling", where the would-be customer knows nothing about the product or service being offered, salespeople are effectively dealing with people who have been warmed up by marketing.

There is much more theory to marketing than there is to selling. Indeed, extensive attention is devoted to it on MBA and other business courses and some business schools – notably the Kellogg School of Management at Chicago's Northwestern University – have made their reputation through it.

Kellogg is the home of Philip Kotler, the doyen of marketing academics. To him, marketing is at the heart of business. A lot of us meet needs but businesses are set up to do it profitably. Good marketing, he believes, leaves little selling work to be done.

WHO SAID IT

"Good companies will meet needs; great companies will create markets."
– **Philip Kotler**

So what is good marketing? It is a range of activities ranging from assessing and analysing potential markets, researching customers and responding to their needs, to telling them what is available through such means such as advertisements and promotions.

The techniques most widely used in the early part of the marketing process are the SWOT analysis and Perceptual

Mapping. A SWOT – Strengths, Weaknesses, Opportunities and Threats – was developed in the 1960s by a team at Harvard. It involves drawing a cross with observations listed under each quadrant heading (see below). It has been widely used in strategic analysis, particularly famously by the US industrial giant General Electric, but is especially useful when assessing whether a product can be launched in certain markets. Perceptual Mapping also involves drawing a cross, although in this case the choice of variables is almost limitless. The technique is used to spot possible gaps in the market.

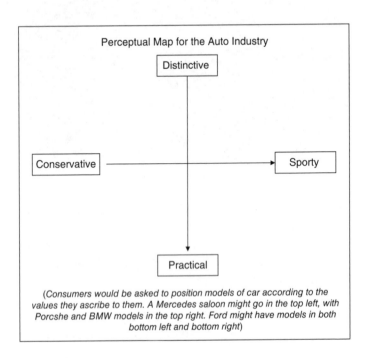

Perceptual Map for the Auto Industry

Distinctive

Conservative → Sporty

Practical

(Consumers would be asked to position models of car according to the values they ascribe to them. A Mercedes saloon might go in the top left, with Porcshe and BMW models in the top right. Ford might have models in both bottom left and bottom right)

THE SWOT MATRIX

Strength	Weakness
Opportunity	Threat

Companies seek to find out about their customers and how they can satisfy their needs in a variety of ways, ranging from carrying out market research to running focus groups. But before they do this they are apt to look at their would-be customers and their products or services by reference to the "hierarchy of needs" introduced to the business world in the 1940s by the American manager and academic Abraham Maslow. This is set out in his 1954 book *Motivation and Personality* and is described in the next chapter, under Motivation.

Much marketing activity, especially that involving branding, operates in the area of esteem because it is dealing with people's aspirations and how they want to be seen – wearing the right clothes, shopping at the right shops, driving the right car, etc.

This is carried through into the part of marketing where customers are told about a product or service through advertisements and the like. One of the most obvious examples of this is the advertising campaign for the beauty products group L'Oreal featuring celebrities under the strapline "Because I'm worth it."

Traditionally, such activity was split into "above-the-line" and "below-the-line" advertising. In the first group are television, cinema and radio advertising, advertisements in newspapers, magazines and other forms of print, posters and billboards and many forms of internet advertising. The second category includes brochures, leaflets and other forms of direct mail, direct email and "viral marketing", sales promotions, public relations (such as getting mentioned in newspapers), business cards and headed stationery and internet blogs. But it is increasingly felt that new developments – particularly in the area of social media – are blurring the distinction. Marketers will tend to use a combination of various forms of marketing – to target different audiences or different markets. In the new media, viral marketing and blogging – essentially the technological equivalents of the old word of mouth so valued by marketers because of its perceived impartiality – are seen as especially effective.

Another development has been the rise of cause-related marketing, where businesses form a link with a charity for their mutual benefit – the charity gains funds and the business gains credit for being public spirited. One of the best examples of this is the Product Red campaign launched in 2006 by the rock singer Bono and others to raise funds for the Global Fund to Fight AIDS, Tuberculosis and Malaria. Companies such as Apple and The Gap take part by donating a proportion of the profits from particular goods to the cause. For many companies, such activities are a central component in their corporate social responsibility strategies.

Although the initials are the same, this is not to be confused with Customer Relationship Management. This is the strategy for managing and developing a company's relationship between existing customers or clients and prospects. It started as the name given for software programs supplied by companies such as Oracle, SAP and Salesforce.com but has become much wider in scope and takes in everything the company does to win business. Having originally been made possible by the advent of powerful computers that could sort and analyse customer data, the concept is being taken to fresh levels by new technology, particularly in the area of mobile phones and other portable devices. Companies increasingly use email and text messages to communicate with customers.

However, perhaps the most powerful example of customer relationship marketing remains the Tesco Clubcard, which is widely credited with putting the supermarket chain at the head of its industry. Many retailers use "loyalty cards" to encourage customers to do more business with them, but few exploit them in the way that Tesco does. The company gives shoppers loyalty points that can be redeemed against goods. But it gets back far more in terms of valuable data. It uses this information to improve the offering in the shops that the card holder uses and to target him or her with offers that are more likely to appeal to them.

With information technology and the devices that use it becoming increasingly sophisticated, it can only be expected that marketing will also become cleverer – more targeted, more immediate and more powerful. Those who realise this and act accordingly are likely to gain a significant edge.

At the same time, though, marketers will have to keep a close eye on that most visible aspect of their work – their brands. This is made all the more difficult by the fact that there is little agreement on what a brand actually is. Originally, of course, it was simply a mark on a product that signified where it came from or who owned it. Later it came to be a symbol that was intended to differentiate the goods or services in question from those of competitors. More recently, proponents of brands have started to talk about brands being part of the relationship between supplier and buyer in their efforts to understand why people buy one product or service over another.

What started as a rather dry legal notion of a sign distinguishing the goods of one company from another and offering some kind of guarantee has developed to the point where every business likes to think it has a brand. In fact, brands have become so ubiquitous that some might think that marketing is all about branding. The field has changed considerably since advertising – as portrayed in the television series "Mad Men" – was in its heyday. Then, companies and products acquired brand status through years of effort (often, admittedly, by advertising executives). Lately, they have become more instant. Many – particularly on the high street – suddenly become commonplace and then just as suddenly disappear. Moreover, thanks to globalisation, they become familiar on high streets across the globe. But this presence across the world, along with consumers' growing concerns about how products are made, also poses a threat to brands that those in marketing need to be aware of. Many makers of expensive clothing and electronic goods have been put on the defensive over negative claims about the conditions in which the products are made.

On the other hand, customers' willingness to be associated with brands – through wearing logos, etc as a sort of badge indicating who they are – creates huge opportunities for smart marketers. For example, the footwear and clothing company Timberland seeks to appeal to outdoorsy people by offering products that use organic or recycled materials.

What will not get any easier will be maintaining an integrity between the brand image and what the business actually does.

OPERATIONS

If sales and marketing is at the glamorous end of business, Operations Management is very much at the other extreme. It covers a wide range of activities ranging from raw materials sourcing, through production to the logistics of getting the goods or services into the market. In short, it deals with the nuts and bolts of the business.

How complex it will be will obviously depend upon the nature of the business. In a services firm, for example, it would be relatively straightforward, but in a manufacturing company with sites around the world and markets split between different countries, it would necessarily be more complex. In such a case, there would be extensive procurement activities as well as management of the supply chain and distribution channels. Each part can be a significant undertaking requiring expertise and organisation.

Operations might not have the appeal of some activities, but it is the heart of any business and it is therefore well worth getting to know what goes on there. For this reason, it is another of those fields that has its own syllabus at many business schools.

The basis of the discipline lies in the "scientific management" developed in the early years of the twentieth century by Frederick W. Taylor when he was seeking ways of improving productivity in what were then comparatively new factories.

Since his time, many management initiatives have either begun in or have applied particularly to activities within operations. Among them are the lean manufacturing

WHO YOU NEED TO KNOW
Frederick W. Taylor

Frederick W. Taylor was an engineer and inventor from Philadelphia who is regarded as the father of "scientific management". Set out in his 1911 book, *The Principles of Scientific Management,* his science – which he described as 75% science and 25% common sense – resulted from close examination of what workers did in factories. Having identified each individual task, Taylor reckoned that he could work out the optimum time to complete it, so giving managers the information by which to judge whether a worker was working well or not. So were sown the seeds of the "command and control" approach to management. Henry Ford was perhaps the most famous adopter of this approach to management, using it as the basis for mass production of cars. But the techniques became commonplace in workplaces around the world, inspiring teams of managers armed with clipboards, effectively until information technology changed how people work and brought about a change in management methods.

model associated with Japanese car makers in the 1980s and 1990s; the just-in-time approach to the delivery of parts, which was also central to the success of Japanese car companies; the quality movement and business process re-engineering, the practice of breaking down how a company does things to make it more efficient. As these initiatives suggest, effective operations management requires a disciplined approach to such matters as planning and scheduling. It also rewards those with an eye for detail.

In recent years, much of operations management has become concerned with Outsourcing. This is partly an outgrowth of business process re-engineering (which was described in the Strategy chapter). The benefits are obvious. Companies can concentrate on what they are best at – highly important when competition is intense. They can also hive off activities that they may not be especially good at to organisations that special-ise in them and therefore are better at them. When you add in the fact that such an approach is generally cheaper than keeping it all in-house, it looks like a win-win situation.

But there are potential pitfalls. Having lots of suppliers and partners around the world can become complex to manage and can create a whole new bureaucracy that may eat away at some of the cost savings. In addition, companies can find the logistics an issue if there is some kind of catastrophe. For example, the ash cloud from Iceland that grounded planes in much of Europe in early

2010 caused great problems for many companies with operations spread around the world.

Potentially more serious, though, are the reputational problems that can result if something goes wrong. For instance, many clothing retailers and electronics manufacturers have been caught out by revelations about conditions in factories operated by suppliers. Moreover, the experience of BP has shown that the fact that the oil rig that exploded in the Gulf of Mexico in 2010 was largely operated by contractors did little to reduce public criticism of it or its potential liability for clean-up costs.

INFORMATION TECHNOLOGY

When companies first began to use computers in the middle of the twentieth century few senior executives understood what they did or how they worked and so delegated responsibility for them to a few people perceived to be experts. That was fine when the computers were doing little more than automating what had previously been done by typing pools and filing clerks. Even when business began to make rather extensive use of what came to be known as information technology a few years later it was still largely seen as a rather limited support function that often fell under the responsibility of the finance director.

It is only comparatively recently that the significance of IT has been acknowledged and that the role of IT director or chief information officer has been created. As the technology has become more pervasive – most businesses have had computers on just about every desk for some time – so the role of the IT department has changed. Whereas a lot of the work in this area used to be done either by the IT specialists directly or with their close support, the growing confidence with computers of employees and the fact that the devices are easier to use means that IT is performing a different sort of role. In keeping with the drive for every function to add value to the business, it is being urged to use the technology and its know-how to try to give the business a competitive advantage. As a result, it is no longer confined to a department but – like the technology itself – it is everywhere.

The scope will depend on the business, of course. Companies that are based around technology will find it hard to separate any activities from IT but even for more traditional ones IT is important. As we have seen above, IT plays an important role in sales and marketing in providing information on customers and markets. It also in some cases effectively runs operations through factory automation and the like, and it facilitates the trend towards outsourcing and spreading different operations around the globe by providing the means of communicating with these units.

In addition, it provides much more detailed and timely information for the finance department. It is because of IT, for instance, that companies are able to announce their results much sooner after the end of the accounting period than used to be the case. Some companies have got the gap down to days rather than the weeks it used to take. Moreover, in an era when knowledge is the key it helps companies to codify and store that knowledge and have it readily available so that, as it were, employees know what they know.

As the influence of IT has grown, so has the importance of the executive responsible for it. At the same time, though, this growing influence has made it essential that all managers have some understanding of it. This is putting more pressure on IT specialists since executives want to hear about solutions rather than difficulties and do not want to be "blinded by science". It is certainly true that the more that can be done, the more that is expected.

It is also true that executives feel that IT cannot be a huge expense even if it is running large parts of the business. This is why IT departments are increasingly about managing relationships with outside suppliers and partners as well as different parts of the organisation rather than running banks of servers or mainframe computers in the basement of headquarters, as used to be the case.

Gartner, an organisation that specialises in researching the IT sector, at the end of 2009 highlighted 10 top technologies and trends that "will be strategic for most organisations in 2010". Some of them are already widespread, others less so. The point is that IT is constantly changing

WHO YOU NEED TO KNOW
Don Tapscott

Don Tapscott is a Canadian consultant and author perhaps best known for popularising the term "paradigm shift" in the book of that title which described how society was changing in the digital age. Since then he has written several other books explaining how digital technology is having a profound effect on all our lives. Rather than feeling threatened by these developments, he urges a celebration of the chaos it brings.

As well as writing extensively on the subject, particularly in praise of how young people are using technology, Tapscott carries out extensive research on the impact of the internet and related technologies on business.

He says: "When today's youth enter the workforce they will do so not as ingénues but as authorities. They will find hierarchies in which their boss knows less than they do. They will also find it bizarre how little information sharing goes on, when they are used to exchanging information with strangers online."

– and doing so quickly. Individuals in this area need constantly to keep up to date with new developments and with what competitors are doing – and they need to be able to advise their senior colleagues on what to do.

As David Cearley, vice president and distinguished analyst at Gartner, said when introducing the trends in October 2009:

> "Companies should factor the top 10 technologies into their strategic planning process by asking key questions and making deliberate decisions about them during the next two years. However, this does not necessarily mean adoption and investment in all of the technologies. They should determine which technologies will help and transform their individual business initiatives."

Among the trends that Cearley sees is the growth of Cloud Computing. This is one aspect of another increasingly important topic – Computing as a Service – and, through accessing services via the internet, enables businesses of all sizes to effectively use IT facilities on a pay-as-you-go basis. Similar to this is Managed Hosting, a concept that is sufficiently exciting that among its leading providers are the likes of Amazon.com, Microsoft and Google.

Another trend very much in evidence is the growth of mobile applications. The intense competition between different kinds of smartphones is fuelling a race to

provide the best and easiest to use links between individuals' phones and their work.

Such is the pace of change in IT that if the others –
including Social Computing, or integrating workers'
personal and work technology, green initiatives such as
tools for reducing energy consumption and ever more
advanced Analytical Tools – are not at the time of writing
much in evidence, they soon will be.

HUMAN RESOURCES

Like IT, Human Resources (HR) has developed rapidly
in recent years. It originated at about the cusp of the
nineteenth and twentieth centuries. In Britain, the spur
was the paternalistic working environment at the chocolate maker Cadbury's Bournville factory, while in the
United States there was a reaction against the "scientific
management" principles expounded by Frederick Taylor
in the shape of what became known as the "human relations" movement. This sought to view workers in terms
of their psychology and "fit" with their employers rather
than as interchangeable parts that could be slotted in
anywhere.

Later in the twentieth century large companies on both
sides of the Atlantic, such as the Ford Motor Company
and the Anglo-Dutch oil group Shell started to adopt the
sort of formal selection and training systems used by the

WHO SAID IT

"Hire people who are better than you, and then leave them to get on with it."
– David Ogilvy

armed forces and the British Civil Service. This led to the development that there should be specialist personnel departments at the centre of companies. Personnel gradually gave way to the term "human resources" as, initially at least, large organisations decided that the business strategy could be underpinned by taking a strategic approach to such matters as pay and training. In some cases, the heads of the newly-minted HR departments even won seats on the boards of their companies and worked alongside the chief executive developing the methods for equipping their workforces for delivering the corporate aims. Royal Bank of Scotland's ability to assimilate NatWest after the ambitious takeover of its much larger rival in 2000 is largely attributed to the work of the Scottish institution's HR department led by Neil Roden.

The rising popularity of the term Human Capital at the end of the twentieth century added to the perception of the importance of HR. As more and more companies saw themselves as employing Knowledge Workers, it became clear that greater and more formalised efforts would have to be made to develop such workers. Chicago economist Gary Becker had in the early 1960s used the concept in an economics context to show that people were another means of production where additional investment yielded additional output. Decades later this idea of people as a resource gave rise to the well-meaning comment in countless annual reports that companies' workers were "their greatest assets".

The arrival of the Knowledge Economy in the 1990s led to a change in approach. As set out by Thomas Davenport, who in his book *Human Capital* effectively launched the idea in its current form, in this world the most valuable workers could not be seen as assets. Instead, they were highly mobile free agents whom organisations had to woo with offers of opportunities, development and the rest because in this increasingly competitive world the contributions of such people would make the difference between failure and success. At about the same time, the phrase "The War for Talent" began to appear – initiated reportedly by a McKinsey consultant in 1997 and later the title of a book: *The War for Talent* by Ed Michaels, Helen Handfield-Jones and Beth Axelrod – and the two developments created a fresh demand for human resources strategies.

Just about all large organisations and many smaller ones have well-staffed HR departments with policies and systems for dealing with a wide range of issues relating to employees. These include recruitment, pay and benefits, training and development and performance management.

In some cases the HR department implements such policies itself, in others it plays a supporting role to line managers, while in still others outside organisations deal with aspects of the role, such as pay and benefits and training and development.

COMMUNICATIONS

Communication is a key activity in any business, but especially in large companies listed on stock exchanges. They are required to communicate to investors anything that can have an impact on the performance of the company (and hence the share price). Because of their size, such organisations are also expected to communicate with the public, usually via media, such as broadcast news or newspapers. And, of course, they will also have to communicate with their employees.

Such is the degree of interest in everything these days, the standard is little lower for all kinds of business organisations. People running health authorities or sensitive

WHO SAID IT

"The problem with communication is the illusion
that it has occurred."
– George Bernard Shaw

operations in local authorities such as children's services
are expected to face the press if anything goes wrong.

Such dealings usually involve bad news. But companies
will also want to communicate good news – about new
products or services, about milestones reached or about
special events – to employees, customers and others.

Whatever communication is involved it needs to be consistent and coherent regardless of the audience. The
company can use a variety of methods of communication
– advertising, public relations or some form of new social
media if that is appropriate – but the message must be
the same whatever the medium.

This is especially important at a time when companies
no longer have control of information. Thanks to the
internet, it is easy for critics of the organisation to find

out about its activities and even gain access to internal communications. If that is inconsistent with the story being told outside, the company could soon find itself in trouble.

Another important factor is globalisation and the speed of communication. Something that happens or is said about a company in one part of the world will be known about in another in seconds. In addition, the arrival of 24-hour news services means that the news has much greater chance of reaching more people than was the case just a few years ago.

Perhaps most important, companies cannot really control the flow of information as well as they used to be able to. Blogs, websites and other forms of new media can spread bad news before a company is even aware that something has happened.

In an era when corporate branding and reputation are seen as more crucial than ever, such bad news can be devastating. The growth in popularity of Corporate Social Responsibility – where companies seek to contribute to their communities through charity work, initiatives in disadvantaged countries or areas of their domestic markets or adopt fair trade policies – can also lead to problems for companies because it can lead to them being held to higher standards than was previously the case.

All this creates an important role for corporate communication specialists, who are now required to be as highly professional and expert as their colleagues in other departments. They will be seeking to promote a strong corporate culture and coherent corporate identity, a genuine sense of corporate citizenship and an appropriate and professional relationship with the press, including quick, responsible ways of communicating in a crisis.

To do this, communication specialists should have a thorough understanding of all the tools and technologies at their disposal. After all, how an organisation communicates with its employees, its extended audiences, the press and its customers brings its values to life. For example, if it wants to come across as lively and dynamic it will need to use such methods of communication as Twitter and mobile messaging. On the other hand, if it wishes to put across a more traditional image it might use press advertisements in a serious or sombre style.

Almost inevitably, though, there will be events that a company would prefer not to have to deal with. Disasters, accusations of using child labour and the like can all tax even the best-run organisation. As long ago as 1999 renowned scenario planner Peter Schwartz and colleague Blair Gibb looked at how companies should deal with such eventualities and should seek to avoid them through anticipating things that would concern their customers and the public at large. Understanding what the public expects of companies in the age of globalisation, corporate social responsibility and intense interest in brands is a key part of corporate communication – as is helping companies restore their reputation by smart action.

WHAT YOU NEED TO READ

▶ General business books describe many of the key ideas behind such disciplines as marketing and human resources. But among the sources that are particularly worth consulting in marketing are Philip Kotler's *Kotler on Marketing* (Free Press) and *Brands and Branding* (The Economist/Profile Books) in which Rita Clifton of the Interbrand consultancy and consultant John Simmons with various other writers and practitioners explore one of the most important aspects of modern business. For a fresh take on the area, there is John Grant's *The New Marketing Manifesto: The 12 Rules for Building Successful Brands in the 21st Century* (Orion)

▶ In the area of Operations, the key text is probably Michael Hammer and James Champy's *Reengineering the Corporation* (HarperCollins), although *The Machine That Changed the World* (Rawson Associates/Macmillan) by James Womack, Daniel T Jones and Daniel Roos is a much-quoted study of lean production.

▶ In Human Resources, Thomas O. Davenport's *Human Capital* (Jossey-Bass) helped redefine how companies see their employees. *Growing Talent* (Marshall Cavendish) is a collection of essays by practitioners seeking to grapple with the practicalities of developing employees in the modern workplace.

▶ Peter Schwartz and Blair Gibb's *When Good Companies Do Bad Things* (John Wiley & Sons) is a reminder that business people must always prepare for the unexpected and be able to communicate their response.

IF YOU ONLY REMEMBER ONE THING

As businesses grow the people working there specialise more – but also have to know how their work fits with that of their colleagues.

CHAPTER 7
THE SKILLS

WHAT IT'S ALL ABOUT

- ▶ What You Need To Succeed
- ▶ Managing Time
- ▶ Communicating
- ▶ Developing Yourself
- ▶ Learning to Lead
- ▶ Being Motivated
- ▶ Being Flexible

Success in business requires all the usual attributes: ambition, hard work, enthusiasm, a willingness to please, inquisitiveness and some luck. However, there are some things that individuals can do to help improve their chances. In addition to making a great effort to understand how the particular business in which they are working and the industry in which it sits works, they should either exhibit or develop certain key skills. Some of the most important are dealt with here.

TIME MANAGEMENT

Working in any business – whether in an office, a factory, out in the field or wherever – typically involves dealing with more than one thing at once. In business, most people have to answer to more than one person and also – in the modern streamlined company of today – do several tasks at once.

Add on top of that the distractions that come from modern communications, such as mobile telephones and email, and it is easy to see how people become stressed and find it hard to get through their work.

Fortunately, there are simple skills that can be applied to create order in all this chaos and help the individual get through the day with some degree of satisfaction. There are also plenty of books that offer tips. Two of them are listed below. There are also helpful websites dealing with this and the other skills covered by this chapter.

There are some so-called time-management experts who teach ways of creating time by doing two things at once, such as cleaning your teeth while in the shower. This might shave off a few minutes each day, but – a bit like eating your lunch at your desk – it can actually make life seem more stressed and so have limited effect. The key is to find ways of working more effectively so that work does not take up all your time and so that you get things done.

Samuel A. Malone in *Mind Skills For Managers* suggests it is important to start with objectives because they are motivational. He recommends the mnemonic SMART as a way to remember the key aspects:

> **S**pecific
> **M**easurable
> **A**ttainable
> **R**elevant
> **T**ime bound

Such an approach is good if you are, for example, starting a new job or project and want to set goals so that you can demonstrate progress. Often, though, people simply struggle with dealing with the day-to-day tasks that characterise business life – people to call, reports to write, files to organise, etc.

In such cases, establishing priorities can be useful. There are various ways of setting priorities. One of the most popular is to list work under "must do", "should do" and "nice to do". Alternatively, tasks can be split into "discretionary" and "non-discretionary".

These are more sophisticated versions of simple to-do lists, which even on their own can concentrate the mind on the tasks in hand – as well as providing a psychological boost when items are ticked off.

Another approach is to accept the Pareto principle. This is named after the Italian economist who reckoned that 20% of the Italian population had 80% of the wealth. This is familiar in business as the 80:20 rule and applies to all kinds of situations. If, for example, 20% of the cheques received in the accounts office account for 80% of the total value of remittances it makes sense to concentrate on getting those to the bank early; the smaller cheques can be totted up later without risk of delaying depositing all the cheques in the bank, and so missing out on interest.

WHO SAID IT

"Never do today what you can put off till tomorrow. Delay may give clearer light as to what is best to be done."
– **Aaron Burr**

Mark Forster, author of *Do It Tomorrow and Other Secrets of Time Management,* has a more radical approach. He calls it "the Mañana Principle" or "The art of getting things done by putting it off to tomorrow". A contrast to the usual puritanical attitude that you should not put off until tomorrow what you can do today, this is a deliberate technique for avoiding becoming distracted by or bogged down in all the little things that happen in the course of a business day. It involves collecting all the tasks that come in during the course of the day and bundling them up for action the following day. By putting in the buffer of one day you are creating the ability to plan the work so that you bunch similar tasks together and get through the next day in an organised fashion. As he says, "Our motto becomes: 'Nothing is so urgent that it can't be put off till tomorrow'."

Another rule that needs to be borne in mind is Parkinson's Law – work expands to fill the time available for its completion. To avoid this, set targets for completing work.

It is possible to be too rigorous and uncompromising in dividing up time between tasks. But it is generally reckoned to be a good idea to deal with such matters as phone calls and the modern bugbear, email, in one go rather than sporadically throughout the day. Much time is also wasted on correspondence that is received. One rule of thumb is that each item should be handled only once: it should be dealt with or put to one side so that somebody else can deal with it or it can be dumped. A variant on this is the four Ds – do, delegate, delay and dump.

However, nothing in business takes up time quite like meetings. Surveys are always providing disheartening statistics on how much of the typical manager's life is spent in them. After all, a committee has been described as a group of people who keep the minutes and waste the hours.

The general advice is to avoid all those meetings that you can by delegating attendance to a colleague. Alternatively, create a finish time for yourself by having another commitment following on. If you are chairing a meeting, bear in mind that the length of it will increase in proportion to the number of people present and that disproportionate amounts of time are taken up by the trivial. The best approach is to do as you would with the work day – prioritise items and allow a certain amount of time for each one.

COMMUNICATION

Since so much of business requires people working together – both within their organisations and with those from others – it is obvious that the ability to communicate is an important skill. Indeed, surveys consistently show that it is a top priority among employers.

With the business world becoming ever more complex, it is more important than ever that employees are able to communicate effectively. Increasingly, workers of all levels are expected to make presentations on projects and proposals, so in addition to having good presentational skills they need the ability to write clearly, accurately and effectively.

Fortunately, there are many sources of advice (how-to books and websites) on the nuts and bolts of putting together Powerpoint presentations, crafting press releases and writing business letters. What is more difficult to master is the ability to communicate naturally and confidently all the time rather than just when in formal situations such as meeting rooms or lecture halls.

Communication skills form part of interpersonal skills and how you communicate through the way you speak and listen and through your body language can make a significant difference to how you are perceived. This is important because success in business can depend a lot on how it is felt you get on with people.

It is generally reckoned that the basic components of good communication are clear thinking, clear speaking and clear writing. But it is also true that many people do not pay sufficient attention to listening. Done well it can lead to a better understanding of people and therefore of their needs.

Typically, though, individuals are too busy concentrating on the talking part – especially in meetings – that they do not listen properly.

Another aspect that is given insufficient attention by many is thinking. Patrick Forsyth, an experienced business trainer and consultant, says in *There's No Need To Shout* that whatever form of communication you are engaged in, "remember to think *before* you communicate". Preparation, he adds, is the foundation for effective communication.

Part of the problem, Forsyth suggests, is that we take communication for granted because we do it all the time. Just because most of the time we muddle through, we

WHO SAID IT

"The most important thing in communication is to hear what isn't being said."
– **Peter Drucker**

should not assume that communication is simple, just as we should not assume that because people were apparently listening they have understood the message.

Most of the time, if a message is misunderstood it merely leads to minor issues and the odd disgruntlement. But at others it can lead to a serious disruption to productivity or the quality of the work. That is not the fault of the listener. That is the fault of the speaker.

Clarity of message is especially important in modern organisations that are increasingly spread across the globe and employ people from many different cultures and with many different first languages. In such an environment the potential for misunderstandings is huge. Even if individuals understand the language they may not pick up the nuances of what is being said. It is therefore vital to be precise in the use of language and to leave no room for ambiguity.

Another problem is jargon. This can be acceptable within the organisation, although it can lead to presentations being packed with meaningless terms because such words have become commonplace among colleagues. But it is much less acceptable when dealing with outside audiences, whether they are customers, suppliers or the general public.

The key is to remember that different forms of communication require different approaches. A sales letter will be different from a press release, for example, while a short talk to colleagues in the same team will be different from a full presentation to the company's board. But each case you will need to prepare well and be aware that in part you are also selling yourself. This is especially true of presentations, of course. But even in written communications, the words used and the tone will give people an impression of you that meeting you will not necessarily change. How you communicate is, after all, an expression of your personality and that can make a significant difference to how you get on in business.

DEVELOPMENT

Not so long ago, new recruits to most large companies could expect extensive induction courses and lengthy training programmes often including periods "sitting next to Nellie", as shadowing experienced employees was known. Other courses came at regular intervals as they moved up the organisation.

That is changing. It is not that companies are abandoning training and development. That would be foolish because arguably it is more important now than ever. Among the many factors putting pressure on organisations to increase their activity in this area are the shift to knowledge work, the rapid uptake of new technologies, increasingly intense global competition and shortages of key skills. But the way that training and development is delivered is changing.

According to a report for Britain's Institute for Employment Studies, learning is moving towards a more continuous and social process, where informality replaces the more structured interventions of the past. The need for organisations to adapt and change quickly as the world develops at an ever increasing pace demands different solutions, and organisations are likely to encourage their people to take greater responsibility for their own learning. This informality is likely to be supported by technology, with the role of the line manager becoming increasingly more central to the success of learning initiatives, the report says.

Indeed, this is already happening. Employees at all levels are increasingly demanding that their managers give them opportunities for professional development, while many organisations are actively encouraging their workforces to take the initiative in training and development.

The learning takes various forms. One of them is Action Learning, which involves the participants learning while dealing with real issues in a group rather than sitting in a classroom. The concept was developed by British management thinker Reg Revans, whose view was that action learning harnessed the power of groups to accomplish meaningful tasks while learning. This also fits with the greater emphasis on teamwork that characterises the modern workplace.

Some companies like to characterise themselves as "learning organisations", the idea being that they are continuously developing corporate knowledge and the capabilities of their employees. In such organisations people have a wide choice of skills and knowledge that they can learn on the basis that all learning helps to develop the individual and so make them more valuable to the organisation.

Employees also increasingly recognise that rather than wait for a move up the corporate ladder that might not come they should consider lateral moves to, say, take part in special projects or work more closely with a customer to gain valuable experience for their careers.

However, there are still opportunities for employees to learn off the job. It is just that rather than being conducted in classrooms, the lessons are more likely to be given via computers. Employees tap into a menu of courses selecting those that fit with the personal development plan agreed with their managers and either in break time at work or in the comfort of their home work their way through materials increasingly delivered via the internet. This produces significant cost savings for the company but also allows the employee to tap into a wider range of courses and to study when it suits him or her.

In the best organisations, employees of all levels have their training and development monitored by their manager through means of a personal development plan that may be linked to their performance appraisals. They may also be allocated a mentor to help guide them through how the organisation works and in making career choices.

The problem for many organisations is that business is developing so fast that even the employees most dedicated to learning and development cannot be guaranteed future employment. As a result, some organisations feel it is not worth investing in this way and leave much of the training to the employee. At the same time, many employees recognise that the most effective way of developing themselves and keeping some kind of control over their careers is to move from employer to employer in order to gain extra experience.

LEADERSHIP

Few subjects in business spark as much debate as leadership. Everybody has a view on what makes a great leader or what kind of leader their organisation or any other needs at any given time. And if they don't, there is always a book with some ideas.

Probably as many books have been written about leadership as any other business topic. There are biographies and autobiographies of business leaders as varied as Bill Gates, Jack Welch and Sir Richard Branson that aspirant executives devour presumably in the hope that some of the magic will rub off on them. There are books about sports coaches and team captains, about military leaders and about politicians. Even religious figures merit a mention. And then there are academic volumes postulating all kinds of theories about what kind of leadership works.

WHO YOU NEED TO KNOW
Warren Bennis

Warren Bennis has packed a lot into a long life –
infantry officer in the Second World War, group
dynamics student and futurologist are just some
of his early occupations. But it is as a thinker on
leadership that he is best known and will probably
be remembered. Based for many years in southern
California and a prolific writer, he has charted the
varying approaches to leadership, particularly
among the heads of large corporations. But
throughout it he retains an adherence to the
human approach in the face of much of the
bombastic writing about leaders as sports or
military-type heroes.

Indeed, he has set out four key attributes of
leaders – the pursuit of a vision, the ability to
communicate this, trust and the acknowledgement
of the need to keep learning. "The worst problem
in leadership is basically early success. There's
no opportunity to learn from adversity and
problems," he said.

So, more than 2000 years after the Chinese philosopher Lao Tse wrote about leadership are we any closer to having a clear idea about what leadership is and how it can be developed? The short answer is not really. John van Maurik in *Discovering The Leader In You* points out that the subject remains elusive because "leadership, whether in a political, military or commercial setting, is about emotion. People react to leaders and their approaches in emotional ways."

Others suggest that at least part of the problem might stem from the fact that we misunderstand the role of leaders. Influenced by all the attention given to them in the media and the lavish pay and benefits packages they command, we are encouraged to see the leaders of big companies as some kind of superheroes who will – like their counterparts in Hollywood movies – save the world.

The reality is rather different. Instead of overarching leaders, there are in many organisations people taking responsibility in many places and at many levels. Meanwhile, Warren Bennis, one of the most renowned thinkers on leadership in the 1970s and 1980s, put forward the notion that in many organisations success was due not to the vision and drive of a single person but to the efforts of teams of co-leaders. Pointing to such examples as Steve Ballmer working alongside Bill Gates at computer software company Microsoft and Craig Barrett complementing Andy Grove at the computer chip maker Intel, he and co-author David A. Heenan write in *Co-Leaders. The Power of Great Partnerships* that co-leadership is not a "fuzzy-minded buzzword" but a "tough-minded strategy that will unleash the hidden talent in any enterprise." Bennis and Heenan acknowledge that some organisations – notably those created through mergers – have had joint leaders. But they say this should be the case in "*every* organisation at *every* level".

WHO SAID IT

"More leaders have been made by accident, circumstance, sheer grit or will than have been made by all the leadership courses put together."
– Warren Bennis

The idea of leadership being about more than one person – especially at a time when globalisation requires many points of view – has also been developed by the Center for Creative Leadership in North Carolina. There, researchers developed the idea of "relational leadership", which involves leadership being thought of as a collective phenomenon rather than a single person showing the way.

It also appears that – just as in politics – there are leaders who are right for different times and not so suited to others. Sometimes, organisations need visionary leaders who will drive them on. At others, they need a more reflective personality.

So, there are many definitions of leadership, but what do leaders actually do? Most commentators start by drawing a distinction between leadership and management. Accordingly, John Kotter, author of *The Leadership Factor*, said management was predominantly activity-based and involved planning and budgeting, organising and staffing and controlling and problem-solving. Leadership, on the other hand, was about creating a sense of direction and communicating the vision. John Adair says leading is about giving direction, especially in times of change; inspiring or motivating people to work willingly; building and maintaining teamwork; providing an example; producing a personal output. Management, by contrast, is about running the business in "steady state" conditions; day-to-day administration; organising structures and establishing systems; controlling, especially by financial methods.

Both sets of skills and activities are essential, he adds. "You have to be a manager-leader or leader-manager depending on your specific role and/or level of responsibility in the organisation."

In practical terms, Adair's view is that effective leaders have to think constantly in terms of achieving the task,

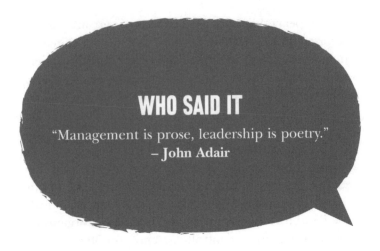

WHO SAID IT

"Management is prose, leadership is poetry."
– **John Adair**

building and maintaining the team and motivating and developing the individual.

MOTIVATION

Talk about motivation in the workplace is common today. However, it was not until the clinical psychologist Frederick Herzberg carried out research among engineers and accountants in Pittsburgh in the United States that there was much science in the area. He and his colleagues simply asked the workers what pleased and what displeased them about their jobs – and came to the conclusion that the motivational elements of work could be split into two categories. There were those serving animal needs (hygiene factors) and those meeting uniquely human needs (motivation factors).

Hygiene factors, which are also known as maintenance factors – include such things as supervision, working conditions, salary, company policies and job security. Workers become dissatisfied when these factors drop below a level the employee considers acceptable, said Herzberg. He added that such factors were insufficient to motivate people to work. That depended on other issues, notably achievement, personal development, job satisfaction and recognition.

The attitudes spawned by Herzberg's research continue today. There are regular surveys showing that employees in the professions in particular are motivated by such matters as doing interesting work, working with other talented people, doing work that they deem to be worthwhile and winning recognition from their peers rather than the money per se.

It is also said to be behind the move towards companies offering "cafeteria" benefits, where employees choose from a menu of options so that they take the benefits that they value rather than a standard package. Likewise, the move towards self-development, career management and self-managed learning fits with this approach.

There is, of course, some overlap between Herzberg's motivation factors and Maslow's hierarchy of needs, described in the illustration below.

WHO YOU NEED TO KNOW
Frederick Herzberg

Frederick Herzberg was a clinical psychologist who – along with the likes of Abraham Maslow and Douglas McGregor – was part of the human relations school in the 1950s. He believed that businesses could be enormous forces for good provided they liberated themselves and their people from an obsession with numbers and got on with expanding individuals' roles within organisations. His identification of the factors that influenced people's behaviour was the root of the idea that companies should motivate people through the job itself rather than through rewards or pressure.

Herzberg followed up the 1959 book *The Motivation To Work* with a 1968 article for the *Harvard Business Review* that has sold more than a million reprint copies. The article – "One more time: how do you motivate employees?" - introduced the acronym KITA (kick in the ass). KITA had three types – negative physical, negative psychological and positive. The last was the best for producing genuine motivation.

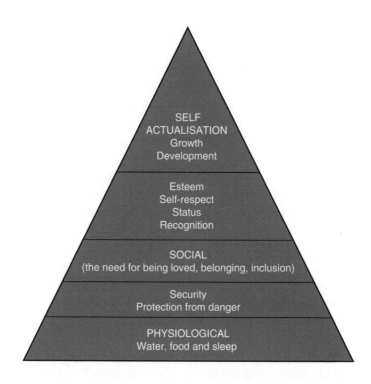

SELF
ACTUALISATION
Growth
Development

Esteem
Self-respect
Status
Recognition

SOCIAL
(the need for being loved, belonging, inclusion)

Security
Protection from danger

PHYSIOLOGICAL
Water, food and sleep

Managers need to realise that each employee will be at a different stage or level in this hierarchy and will need to be motivated accordingly. Bearing this in mind, John Adair sets out six key principles for motivating others:

- ▶ Be motivated yourself
- ▶ Select people who are highly motivated
- ▶ Set realistic and challenging targets
- ▶ Remember that progress motivates
- ▶ Provide fair rewards
- ▶ Give recognition

Inevitably, there will be people who are not so well motivated. It is all very well talking about professionals finding reward in interesting work, but even in this age of the "knowledge economy" there are many people doing boring jobs that they can almost do in their sleep and who probably find whatever motivation they have in life outside work. What do you do about them?

Trainer and coach Mike Leibling in the book *How People Tick* acknowledges that it is difficult, but he urges managers in such situations to ask "the magic question": usually some form of "What needs to happen to …?"

It might not work – at least immediately – but then "by stimulating someone's motivation, curiosity or interest, you might indeed awaken their hunger for learning, self-improvement and progress."

Others argue that in a highly competitive business world merely motivating employees is not enough. Leadership thinker Lance Secretan says: "We have a greater need than motivation – we want to be *inspired*. We are not looking for leaders to *motivate* us so much as we want them to lift our spirits. The real issue has become inspiration." He adds:

> "In a world where great contributors continue to be in short supply, our responsibility is to find the right colleagues to fill these roles and then inspire them so much that they wouldn't even think about leaving

the team, but instead, use their imagination to entice their friends to join them, thus filling out our team's full complement and potential."

FLEXIBILITY

The business environment is so complex and fast-moving that increasingly only the fleet-footed look likely to prosper. Challenges come from every direction, some expected, others completely unpredictable. As Andy Grove, the former head of the computer chip maker Intel, famously remarked (and called his autobiography) "Only the paranoid survive".

It naturally follows, then, that organisations have to be flexible, adaptable and pragmatic. It is no longer sensible – or indeed possible – to set out more than a rough strategy for the next five years, so companies have to be prepared to have a look at markets or industries and ramp up their presence if it goes well or withdraw if it does not.

It also naturally follows that those who work in modern organisations – whatever their sector and wherever they are – must be prepared to be flexible and adaptable, too. In many cases, this will mean that they will not have the career that they thought they were going to have. For many years, it has been glibly stated that the modern employee will have several career changes over their working life. This still does not look that likely in all but the most extreme cases. But it is true that the nature of the work they do will change considerably more than it did for previous generations. Modern workers are already working harder than their forebears – and will continue to do so for a lot less security. Indeed, one of the ways in which companies have responded to the need to be more flexible is by shedding many of their permanent employees in favour of temporary workers that they can take on and let go as and when they need to. And whereas they used to do this primarily with lower-ranked employees they are increasingly taking this approach to more senior roles, too.

Many of these employees feel threatened by this approach and hanker for the "good old days" of moving up the corporate ladder. But many others enjoy working on projects in this way, arguing that it makes work more interesting and stops them getting stale as well as giving them the opportunity to take breaks between assignments. As a result, rather than wait to be taken on and dropped by companies, they have consciously embraced the freelance life and set themselves up as free agents.

Most of these interim managers will have particular skills – as finance or human resources specialists, say – that organisations value and can draw on as the need arises. Indeed, finding themselves constantly working in fresh situations can help them hone these skills to a very high level of expertise.

But organisations still rely on a cadre of individuals to remain in place and provide continuity whatever is going on. These individuals will have to be masters of adaptability and flexibility, prepared to turn their hands to a range of tasks while also ensuring that they are still expert at their original skill, whether it be information technology, human resources or whatever.

Much will depend on the pragmatism of individuals. Obviously, those that are best at embracing change will be best suited to this way of doing things. But it also has to be realised that a lot will also depend on the approach taken by the organisation itself. Management thinker and writer Costas Markides says in a contribution to the *Financial Times Handbook of Management* that "a firm must be able to identify, early enough, changes in its environment; it must then have the cultural readiness to embrace change and respond to it; and it must have the requisite skills and competences to compete in whatever environment emerges after the change." In other words, companies should prepare by preparing their workforces.

This will never be the whole answer, though. As in anything else, those that succeed best will be those that make it their own business to prepare themselves as best they can for every eventuality – by showing initiative, by revealing a readiness to approach tasks in fresh ways and by acquiring extra knowledge in their own time.

Fortunately, those entering the workforce now could be well-suited to this new environment – with a few adjustments. Bruce Tulgan, a trainer and author, argues that Generation Yers (those born in 1978 or later) are in many ways best suited to what is going on in business. They have been brought up by parents, teachers and others to believe they can do anything. "And they believe it – they are overflowing with self-esteem," he says, adding that their facility with information technology makes them would-be experts on just about everything and they are mastering a just-in-time approach to learning and development. Managers just need to stop trying to please them all the time and set stiff challenges. "Generation Y is the most high-maintenance workforce in history, but they also have the potential to be the most high-performing if they are managed the right way," he says.

WHAT YOU NEED TO READ

▶ Time management attracts much attention and there are many books devoted to it. Among the more useful are Mark Forster's *Do It Tomorrow* (Hodder & Stoughton) and Samuel A. Malone's *Mind Skills for Managers* (Gower).

▶ Similarly, there is no shortage of guides to communicating. Again, Malone has useful tips, while Patrick Forsyth speaks sense in *There's No Need To Shout* (Marshall Cavendish).

▶ Leadership is an industry all of its own, complete with a specialist set of gurus. *John Adair's 100 Greatest Ideas For Effective Leadership and Management* (Capstone) and *Living Leadership. A Practical Guide for Ordinary Heroes* (FT/Prentice Hall) by George Binney, Gerhard Wilke and Colin Williams are useful starting points. Warren Bennis is one of the great names of this field and has sought to counter the idea of the mighty leader with *Co-Leaders. The Power of Great Partnerships* (John Wiley & Sons), a book written with David A. Heenan.

▶ John van Maurik's *Discovering The Leader In You* (McGraw-Hill) offers tips for individuals seeking to make their mark.

▶ On motivation, the obvious place to start is with Frederick Herzberg's *The Motivation To Work* (John Wiley & Sons), while Andrew Mayo updates the notion in *The Human Value of the Enterprise* (Nicholas Brealey).

▶ One of the first to see the sort of direction in which modern work was heading was Daniel

Pink, whose *Free Agent Nation* (Business Plus) is a bible for freelancers and other flexible workers everywhere.

▶ There are also useful websites, including www.mindtools.com, www.fastcompany.com and www.Time-Management-Guide.com.

IF YOU ONLY REMEMBER ONE THING

The modern employee needs to be flexible and adaptable and acquire plenty of skills.

CHAPTER 8
SUCCESS

WHAT IT'S ALL ABOUT ➡

- ▶ Criteria for Success
- ▶ New Ideas of Success
- ▶ Emerging Markets

WHAT IS SUCCESS?

It is, of course, a rare business that does not wish to succeed. Business is far too much work to be embarked upon without a determination to make a go of it. But there are many views of success and an increasing number of approaches to achieving it. Indeed, with the rise in the number of social enterprises and not-for-profits on the one hand and the increasing commercial acumen displayed by some charities and government bodies, it can be hard to see the difference between the two.

The chances are that this blurring will intensify as governments around the world start to scale back their activities in areas such as welfare, care provision and the community, and businesses move into the space vacated. The increasingly complex and competitive environment so often described by commentators might make it a lot easier to fail than to succeed, but – thanks in part to trends like these – there are perhaps more opportunities for business than ever before. And a wider range of business models.

Until comparatively recently, it was all so simple. The business of business was to increase profits and so improve returns for shareholders. And a business that survived for a number of years by making increasing amounts of money and expanding was seen to be a success. A business that could boast of having been around for many years was seen as especially successful

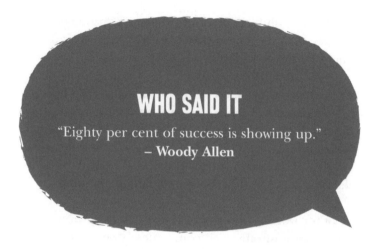

WHO SAID IT

"Eighty per cent of success is showing up."
– **Woody Allen**

and therefore a safe bet to work for, sell things to or to buy things from.

NEW DEFINITIONS OF SUCCESS

Now, it is rather more complex. Having learned from the experiment in the "New Economy" that was bound up in the dot.com boom of the late 1990s and early 2000s, business people realise that they have to eventually make a profit – or make sufficient impact that somebody will take them over in the hope that they will one day make money.

In the technology field, in particular, there are many examples of businesses that may not have succeeded in the conventional sense but could still be seen to have been successful in, say, introducing consumers to a market or indicating a direction in which an industry might be headed.

At the same time, succeeding by financial criteria is no longer enough. Companies also need to satisfy various other criteria. For example, the UK Corporate Governance Code states that the board of a company "should set its values and standards and ensure that its obligations to its shareholders and others are understood and met".

In other words, the sorts of issues that were previously the concern of only such companies as beauty products company The Body Shop in Britain and ice cream maker Ben & Jerry's in the United States have become mainstream.

This is because profits and values need not be incompatible. This is even more apparent when it comes to the environment. Companies have realised that doing something positive for the environment, such as reducing energy use, can also make them more profitable by cutting costs.

Of course, such decisions are easier to make when a company is owned by its managers rather than by outside shareholders. But it is encouraging that even big, publicly-owned businesses are realising that "doing the right thing" and making a profit do not have to be incompatible. It is notable that there are several instances of large companies taking over smaller, quirky, cause-led businesses and apparently leaving them to do their own thing. Examples include the Anglo-Dutch consumer goods company Unilever acquiring Ben & Jerry's, cosmetics company L'Oreal Group's acquisition of The Body Shop and Cadbury's purchase of the premium organic chocolate company Green & Black's.

This is not entirely revolutionary, of course. Companies as varied as the long-established US electronic products maker Hewlett-Packard and the British chocolate maker Cadbury have long histories of being benevolent employers, responsible citizens – and highly successful businesses.

Hewlett-Packard is one of several companies – including the industrial group 3M, the hotels chain Marriott and the pharmaceutical company Merck – featured in *Built To Last*, the 1994 book by Stanford University's James C. Collins and Jerry I. Porras that set out to identify the common characteristics of businesses that remained successful over a significant length of time. Their findings are deceptively simple and include the importance of having a purpose beyond making a profit and – fundamentally – aligning those aspirations with genuine actions. Along the way they demolish such myths as the notion that successful businesses are based on a great idea and the belief that they must be led by charismatic leaders. At the end of the book, Collins and Porras insist that, although they believe their thesis explains the past success of certain businesses, their findings are perhaps even more relevant in the 21st century.

CORPORATE BONDING

For example, successful companies will embrace the idea of taking two apparently contradictory approaches simultaneously so that, for instance, they "become increasingly fanatical about preserving their core ideology *and* becoming increasingly aggressive in granting operational autonomy to individual employees". In flatter, more decentralised businesses, employees will be less likely to be controlled through hierarchies, systems, budget and the rest. Instead, they will be motivated more by an increasingly ideological "corporate bonding glue", they maintain.

This idea that people want to work for companies that stand for something has been gathering pace – and is likely to continue to do so. Since the later years of the 20th century, large businesses in particular have sought to fend off concerns about their power and influence by stressing their commitment to interests other than their shareholders. Companies began to publish environmental and social audits alongside their traditional financial reports and there was increasing talk of "stakeholders", "licences to operate" and the "triple bottom line" of "people, planet, profit" as executives effectively acknowledged the expanding role of business in everyday lives.

Again, such actions were not entirely new. John Micklethwait and Adrian Wooldridge report in *The Company* that even in the early years of the 20th century big companies were adopting measures that would now be termed corporate social responsibility. For example, the retail and mail order company Sears Roebuck established a pension fund for its employees, while US Steel established various employee welfare programmes and company towns were built on the basis that "well-housed and well-educated workers would be more efficient than their slum-dwelling, feckless contemporaries".

SOCIAL ENTERPRISE

Equally, though, there has been a growing realisation that the energy, ideas and wealth of business can have a highly positive effect on society. It has long been accepted that it is in the interests of businesses for the communities in which they operate to be prosperous. But there is an increasing desire to become involved and to make things change. This is partly a response to the efforts of organisations like Britain's Business in the Community programme, which has encouraged businesses of all kinds to become involved – as the name suggests – in the world around them. The result is that the public has begun to associate certain businesses with good causes and, perhaps more significantly, employees have started to feel better about being in business in general and about working for certain companies in particular.

More direct action is being taken by an increasingly common brand of business known as the "social enterprise". Like corporate social responsibility, the idea of the social business has been around for some time. The origins go back at least as far as the mid-19th century, when a workers' co-operative was set up in Rochdale to provide high-quality affordable food for factory workers. However, in the UK and elsewhere there has been a resurgence in recent years, with various different approaches, including co-operatives, community enterprises and enterprising voluntary organisations, coming together to tackle such issues as health and welfare that were previously largely the preserve of charities. It can be argued that the popularity of social enterprise – a 2007 poll by YouGov found that 60% of the British public would prefer their local services to be run by a social enterprise instead of the Government, or a traditional private business or charity – is an indication of faith in business as a way of getting things done.

Even the financial crisis has not halted this trend. Indeed, another report, a State of Social Enterprise Survey published in November 2009, found that in the wake of the recession social enterprises were twice as confident of future growth as typical small and medium-sized enterprises. In addition, 56% of them had increased their turnover over the previous year, with fewer than 20% seeing it go down. By contrast, 28% of all SMEs saw turnover increase and 43% experienced a fall.

Indeed, it appears that the crisis has made many in business more determined than ever to show how business can be a force for good. At the World Economic Forum in Davos in 2008, Bill Gates, who as head of Microsoft attracted a fair share of brickbats from opponents of big business, launched what he called "a new approach to capitalism". This was the starting point for *Creative Capitalism*, a book of essays by him, the investor Warren Buffett and others, which was collected by the journalist Michael Kinsley.

A similar theme is proposed by Muhammad Yunus, founder of Grameen Bank, the microcredit organisation that has enabled poor women in Bangladesh to gain the access to finance needed to set up their own businesses. In his book *Creating a World Without Poverty* he sets out to urge readers to harness the power of the free market to solve the problems of poverty, hunger and inequality.

Certainly, much of the energy of design companies and others involved with innovation and creativity goes into what could be termed social enterprise. And this is being encouraged by people going into business. That 2007 YouGov survey found that 30% of respondents would like to work for a social enterprise – compared with 16% opting for a traditional business, 13% choosing a public organisation and 13% a traditional charity.

DIFFERENT APPROACHES

At the same time, though, there is a growing feeling that the Anglo-Saxon way is not the only route to success.

Spates of corporate scandals every few years lead many to question whether what has been termed the "American Enterprise Model" should continue to dominate capitalism. Donald Kalff, an executive and business school academic, has proposed in his book *An UnAmerican Business* a European alternative on the basis that the American way of doing business is not necessarily as efficient as is supposed. Writing before the economic crisis in the Eurozone, of course, he argued that Europe was "large and strong enough to go its own way and to become the most successful region in the world". As part of this, he suggested that there were "huge opportunities" in taking a different approach to such areas as corporate ownership, governance, management, performance evaluation and executive remuneration.

There are signs of such thinking in the continued importance – particularly in Germany and other parts of continental Europe – of family businesses and privately-owned firms. In addition, there is renewed interest in co-operatives and mutuals. The latter had been closely associated with the building society movement, but largely disappeared in the boom years of the financial markets at the end of the 1990s through converting to companies under pressure to release value – only to be for the most part taken over by larger companies.

At the same time, certain large European businesses have continued to operate in quite different ways to typical US businesses. For example, efforts are made to maintain links with the original sites of the business, employees are involved in the management through works councils and financing is often arranged through long-established links with regional banks rather than via more sophisticated routes.

EMERGING MARKETS

However, there is no real evidence of a distinctive European brand of capitalism. On the other hand, the rise in importance of quite different sorts of countries – especially China and India – could yet bring about change in the way that business is conducted. At the very least there are likely to be different types of company to work for – meaning that employees of all types and at all levels should be prepared to be adaptable.

For example, Adidas of Germany and Nike of the United States have been leaders in the sportswear industry for many years. In 2008, their global revenues were $ 15.9 bn and $ 18.6 bn respectively. But they could soon give way to a business that many will not have heard of – Li Ning. This is China's largest sportswear company and is owned by Li Ning, who was a gymnastics star of the 1984 Los Angeles Olympics. According to Edward Tse (in his book *The China Strategy*), Li Ning was in 2008 much smaller than the well-established brands, with sales of more than $ 980m. But it was growing faster – with sponsorship of basketball in several countries and, of course, its founder's appearance lighting the torch at the opening ceremony of the Beijing Games. This was serious enough for Adidas and Nike – one more symbol of China's declaration of intent to make it on the world stage. But, as Tse makes clear, there are hundreds of thousands of entrepreneurs keen to make it like Li Ning.

China's increasing involvement in the economies of the leading industrial countries in many ways might follow the western model – through investments in companies and financial institutions and the rest. But there are also signs of a different approach. Tse describes how some of the country's best companies have "a sense of purpose that extends far beyond simply making money for their owners". They want to be profitable, world-class companies but they also want to make a mark on the world for China and they want to be influenced by the world.

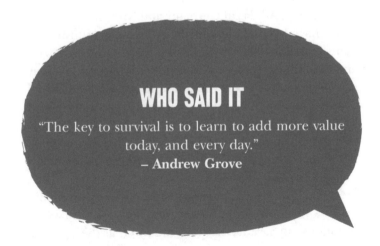

WHO SAID IT

"The key to survival is to learn to add more value today, and every day."
– Andrew Grove

India, too, is seeing rapid developments. It has for a while been moving from being a centre for finance, customer service and other activities outsourced from large companies and has started to develop its own businesses in such fields as IT services and technology products. In *The India Way*, Peter Cappelli, Harbir Singh, Jitendra Singh and Michael Useem of Wharton Business School explain how a group of companies in India is experiencing huge growth in the midst of a global recession. They identify four "principal practices" – holistic employee engagement, improvisation and adaptability of managers, creative value delivery to customers, and a sense of broad mission and purpose. This last is particularly striking – and important, given the region's huge social problems.

WHO SAID IT

"I want to work for a company that contributes to and is part of the community. I want something not just to invest in. I want something to believe in."
– **Anita Roddick**

One of the companies featured in the book is HCL Technologies, a huge information technology services

business with 55000 employees spread across 18 countries and serving such well-known international clients as
the aircraft maker Boeing, the internet business Cisco
and the pharmaceuticals company Merck. In 2005, the
company appointed as chief executive Vineet Nayar, who
had earlier created the unit that had helped convert the
business from a hardware operation into a services
organisation.

Nayar took the company further away from outsourcing
in search of more lucrative work by getting closer to existing customers and better meeting their unique needs,
"another example of the innovativeness and adaptability
that are part and parcel of the India Way approach to
business strategy," according to Cappelli et al.

Nayar's account of this journey is set out in his own book,
Employees First, Customers Second. The title is a reflection
of Nayar's genuine belief that top-rank customer service
can only be delivered if the employees responsible for
delivering that service have all the resources and autonomy they need to get the job done.

The company's 20% growth between the financial years
2008 and 2009 at a time of global recession is proof that
the strategy is working for HCL, says Nayar. It is also
significant for western companies. As Nayar points out,
companies like HCL are starting to have an impact on
the global stage because they can deliver high value at
highly competitive prices through being innovative in
finding ways of becoming more efficient and so more

productive. The result is that old western-style business models and pricing points will no longer work, not just in countries like India and China, but also in their domestic markets as well.

Another feature of the India Way is engagement with employees. This is true not only at HCL but also at many other Indian businesses, where executives pay close attention to employee issues because they believe it drives competitive advantage. But HCL – with its turning upside down of the organisational pyramid so that management is at the bottom supporting front-line employees and its open-books approach – is even by these standards unusual.

It is reminiscent of the leadership approach of a businessman in another so-called emerging market – Brazil.

Now that Indian and Chinese companies are starting to play a significant part in world business (rather than just a supporting role as suppliers of low-cost labour), this sort of approach is likely to become more mainstream. All the research about the generation of people now entering the workforce suggests that they are more likely to respond to this style of management rather than the command-and-control approach that still persists in many places despite advances in technology and changes in social morals. As a result, companies wanting to attract the best people are likely to at least consider becoming more open in their management style.

WHO YOU NEED TO KNOW
Ricardo Semler

Ricardo Semler shot to worldwide fame in 2001 with his book *Maverick*, in which he describes how he made his family business Semco more transparent and more accessible at the same time as improving its fortunes. Starting by firing 60% of top management, he re-organised the company so that small teams were responsible for all levels of the production process. Each group also had control of its own budgets and targets. Apparently, as a result of stripping out authority and introducing new ways of working, productivity soared.

The real test came in the recession of the 1990s, but so committed was the workforce by then that severe cost-cutting measures were agreed. Encouraged by this attitude, Semler took worker empowerment even further, so that teams could recruit and fire their bosses. There were no secretaries, no job titles and all salaries were disclosed. His approach of really "empowering" employees so that they could choose the work that best suited them has inspired many other managers.

But empowering employees will only really bring results if the employees are informed about all aspects of the business and the environment in which it operates. Which makes the need for a book like this all the more apparent.

WHAT YOU NEED TO READ

▶ One of the best-known analysts of success in business is James C. Collins, who alone and with Jerry I. Porras in such books as *Built To Last* (Century) and *Good To Great* (Harper Business) has set out "successful habits". But with success increasingly coming in different shapes and sizes, it is worth looking at other approaches. Robert Reich, a member of former president Bill Clinton's cabinet, examines the role of big business in society in *Supercapitalism* (Icon Books), while *Creating a World Without Poverty* (publicaffairs) contains microcredit pioneer Muhammad Yunus's views on the role of social businesses, and *People, Planet, Profit* (Kogan Page) by Peter Fisk is a practical guide to introducing sustainable business practices.

▶ *Googled* (Virgin) by Ken Auletta and *Free* (Random House) by *Wired* editor-in-chief

Chris Anderson describe how mastery of technology is key to a coming new business order. However, there is another dimension to this – the Asian aspect. Many books are attempting to describe what is going on, but *The India Way* (Harvard Business Press) by Peter Cappelli and others and Edward Tse's *The China Strategy* (Basic Books) do it in a compelling fashion.

IF YOU ONLY REMEMBER ONE THING

The modern business is a place of serious threats and huge opportunities. Survival will depend on courage and flexibility.

ACKNOWLEDGEMENTS

I would like to thank the many business people, consultants and commentators who have over the past couple of decades shared their time and wisdom with me. Their insights have been invaluable.

Thanks, too, to my family for putting up with the stresses and strains associated with the writing of this book. In particular, my daughter Lucie and her technological know-how saved an oldster from embarrassment when the deadline was looming.

Finally, the team at John Wiley has been helpful, supportive and understanding.

INDEX